➤ I've heard you can save a lot of money by selling a house yourself. How do I decide whether to work with a real estate broker or put a FOR SALE BY OWNER sign in my front yard?

➤ I'm confused. Is there a difference between a real estate *broker,* a real estate *agent,* and a real estate *salesperson*?

➤ What is a disclosure statement? Will a good real estate agent offer to show it to me?

➤ When do I need to use a real estate attorney?

➤ What should I look for in a buyer's inspection?

➤ I'm desperate! I can't get a lender to loan me the money I need to buy a house. What do I do?

➤ Can I improve my credit rating so that I can get the mortgage I want at the lowest possible cost?

➤ My neighbor told me that real estate commissions are *negotiable*. Really?

➤ Do real estate agents get kickbacks or finders' fees for making referrals to specific lenders?

➤ What are the telltale signs of a good, responsible agent?

WHAT THE "EXPERTS" MAY *NOT* TELL YOU ABOUT™ BUYING—OR SELLING—A HOME OR APARTMENT . . . COULD LEAVE YOU HOMELESS!

In this book, every question you will ever ask about buying a home is answered. Now you can know what the insiders know, avoid costly mistakes, and get the beautiful house you want!

WHAT THE "EXPERTS" MAY NOT TELL YOU ABOUT™ ...

Buying a House or Apartment

DAN RAMSEY

WARNER BOOKS

NEW YORK   BOSTON

The techniques and methods described in this book are the result of the author's experience in working with certain materials. Care should be taken to use the proper materials and tools as advised by the author. The information in this book is as up to date as possible; however, it is sold with the understanding that real estate laws, construction and zoning codes, etc., are often subject to new and changing interpretations, government rulings, and legislation. The reader should consult with a professional regarding specific questions. The publisher and the author will assume no liability for any injury or damage to persons or property which may result from the use or application of any of the contents of this book.

The title of the series What the "Experts" May Not Tell You About . . . and the related trade dress are trademarks owned by Warner Books, Inc., and may not be used without permission.

Warner Books

Time Warner Book Group
1271 Avenue of the Americas, New York, NY 10020
Visit our Web site at www.twbookmark.com.

Printed in the United States of America

First Printing: July 2004

10 9 8 7 6 5 4 3 2 1

Library of Congress Cataloging-in-Publication Data

Ramsey, Dan
    What the "experts" may not tell you about buying a house or apartment / Dan Ramsey.
        p.   cm.
    Includes bibliographical references and index.
    ISBN 0-446-69092-9
    1. House buying.   2. Condominiums.   I. Title.
HD1379.R365 2004
643'.12—dc22   2004001969

Book design by Stratford Publishing Services

Acknowledgments

Thanks to Denise Gentry, of Beverly Sanders Realty Company. Denise is one of the most professional agents I've ever worked with. That's why I turned to her when I began writing this book. I needed straightforward advice on the latest real estate market conditions. Besides my own real estate sales experience as an agent, a buyer, and a seller, I've authored three books on real estate transactions. But the market changes. Denise brought me up to date as well as offered many practical insider's tips to share with you in the coming pages. Thanks, Denise!

Thanks to those who first taught me real estate: Lou Hatch, Frank Webber, and Lloyd Nelson. They showed me that hard work and professionalism pay off.

And thanks to the numerous *un*professional real estate experts who showed me over the years what *not* to do—and why. I met them during my own career as a real estate agent as well as during the process of buying and selling seven homes in four states over nearly thirty years. Many of these agents are probably selling used cars today—so beware.

Last, but first, thanks to *you,* the reader. It's my sincere hope that your life will be more enjoyable because of what you learn in the coming pages.

Contents

Introduction

*M*ore than six million homes, condos, co-ops, and other residential properties are bought in the United States every year. At an average price of $200,000, that adds up to more than *$1 trillion*! How much of that money do you think is wasted on bad advice, poor communication, ineptitude, dishonesty, and just plain lack of knowledge? *Too* much!

When I first became a licensed real estate agent more than twenty-five years ago, I discovered that there are many so-called experts—agents, brokers, lenders, lawyers, and others—passing off sloppy work as "good enough." They are paid well to help with the largest purchase that most people make, yet they often cut corners, ignore warning signs, and forget to give buyers and sellers very important information. Yes, there are a number of people out there intentionally stealing from buyers and sellers, but the bigger problem is the large body of self-styled real estate experts who think they are on the up and up, but don't do what they are paid to do. No, it's not all of them, but it's certainly *too many* of them.

What can you do about it? You can learn how the real estate market is *supposed* to work. You can discover how to hire the best and work around the rest—or do it yourself. You can be a smart real estate buyer!

Why Experts Won't Tell You

So why would a real estate agent or other professional *not* tell you something you need to know? Many reasons:

➤ The expert doesn't know, either.

➤ The expert hasn't taken the time to find out.

➤ The expert knows but doesn't want you to know.

➤ The expert doesn't understand what you're asking.

THE EXPERT DOESN'T KNOW

What credentials do you need to become a real estate agent? Not many, really. Each state sets its own standards, but other than not having a criminal record all that is required in many states is that the candidate take a class or two and pass a multiple-choice test. The candidate can study numerous books on real estate law and marketing *or* can simply sign up for a crash course on how to take the state real estate exam. It's not always easy for you to figure out who really studied and has the knowledge you need and who just crammed—unless you know what questions to ask (chapter 6).

THE EXPERT HASN'T FOUND OUT

The most important qualification a real estate expert needs is *self-management*—knowing how to best spend her or his time. Not everyone has this skill. After a few months or a few years, those without this skill drift back to jobs where someone tells them when to get to work, how much time to take for lunch, and when to go home. Meantime, these agents-adrift can waste other people's time and money because they haven't wisely used their time to find out what buyers need to know. They would much rather chat on the phone with friends, take long lunch hours, or knock off early because it's a beautiful day—anything except do homework on behalf of their clients. You'll see what they are supposed to do in chapter 5.

THE EXPERT DOESN'T WANT YOU TO KNOW

Here's one thing many agents won't tell you: You don't *need* them to purchase a residence or other real estate! You can do this yourself, following my instructions in part 3 of this book, "Buying a Home Without an Agent."

In addition, an agent may not want you to know the answer to a very specific question: "What do you know about so-and-so?" or "Have property values gone up or down in the last few years?" As you will learn in this book, most real estate agents don't really work for you; they work for the seller. They cannot, by law, tell you everything the seller or another agent has told them. And they can't tell you bad things about another agent. So how are you going to get the answers you want? Chapter 7 will tell you how.

One more important thing: Frankly, many experts are less than honest because they are afraid of being sued. In this litigious society, saying the wrong thing—or even the truth—can land a person in court. That gets expensive and ends careers. So an agent or other real estate expert may not tell you because of the fear of lawsuits.

THE EXPERT DOESN'T UNDERSTAND YOUR QUESTION

What is heard is not always what is said. It's a primary law of communication. Sometimes it's an intentional misunderstanding, and sometimes it's because you're not speaking the same language.

The first four chapters of this book, part 1, will bring you up to speed on how the real estate market works and how to speak the language. In fact, the entire book is written to help you understand the language of real estate without sitting through boring lectures. I'll cover terms in context so you can build your vocabulary. Most important, you'll be able to word your questions correctly to get the right answers.

How about those few dishonest real estate folks out there? How can you identify and avoid them? I'll show you how.

Why I *Will* Tell You

Why am I telling you this? First off, I no longer make my income as a real estate agent. I'm now a general building contractor and a writer. So I don't have to "make nice" about agents, brokers, lenders, title and escrow officers, sellers, and other real estate experts. I can tell you what I know and what you should hear rather than what others want me to tell you so I can get my commission. You've bought (or were given) this book, so I'm already paid. I can tell you what your real estate agent or other pro may not, cannot, or will not tell you.

Real estate is an education. You get the education, and the teachers get your tuition. The price of this book is tuition that can save you many thousands of dollars in unnecessary costs when buying real estate. You don't want to learn the hard way how to find and use a good real estate agent—or how to do it yourself.

As you'll learn, the key to getting the most value from a real estate transaction is knowledge. When you get done reading this book, you'll know more about real estate than some real estate "experts." And you'll know how to hire *real* experts to help you. They are out there, believe me. And they're willing to work hard and smart for you. You'll also learn how to save money by handling some or all of the transaction yourself.

How to Use This Book

Now let me tell you how to get the most you can from this book.

First, don't be afraid to write in it. Use the inside covers, insert sticky notes, or start a Buyer's Notebook so that you'll have the most important facts where you can quickly get at them.

Second, check out the table of contents. You'll see that this book is broken down into three parts:

➤ What You Need to Know *Before* Buying Real Estate

➤ Getting the Most from a Real Estate Agent

➤ Buying a Home Without an Agent

Third, scan the chapters. The titles will tell you that we're going to cover lots of ground—everything from finding qualified experts to moving into your new house, condo, or co-op apartment. Along the way, I'll offer you some clarifying definitions, insider's tips, and warnings, like these:

Lingo

Real estate words you really should know, defined and explained so you can recognize and use them.

Insider's Tip

Especially valuable information that can save you time, money, and effort when buying your residence.

Pitfall

Things to watch for to make sure you don't get robbed. Learn from others' mistakes.

Finally, feel free to use the real estate glossary and resource appendices at the back of this book. They are valuable investments in your real estate education.

PART ONE

What You Need to Know *Before* Buying Real Estate

CHAPTER 1

It All Boils Down to Property Rights

*N*obody *really* owns property. They actually own the *right to use* property. Some property rights include living on it, using the water on it, owning any minerals or oil under it, and even the right to sell some of these rights to others. And it's these property *rights*—not the property—that get bought and sold in the marketplace.

Unfortunately, these rights can get confusing as owners sell off some and not others, forget to register (record) a sale, get a loan against the property, or give rights away to heirs. That's where things can get muddy. You come along ready to buy, but you may not be getting the rights you think you bought. That's where understanding property rights is really important to buyers. Most real estate agents know this, too, but some forget—or they assume that you know. A few don't care. So the first thing you need to know before buying real estate is how property rights work and how they are transferred between buyers and sellers.

What Is Property?

Just about anybody can own property, including individuals, groups (couples or corporations), and even governments. Fortunately, property rights are about the same for everyone. These rights are defined by state laws, but most states have similar laws about real estate, so most of the terms used here and by real estate professionals are the same. I'll tell you about state differences later in this chapter.

Real property, as you now know, isn't really dirt and a residence. It's the *right* to use a specifically defined piece of real estate.

Lingo

Real property is the right to use real estate. *Real estate* is the land and everything attached to it. *Personal property* is everything not attached to the land. The right of real property extends from the center of the earth to the end of the earth's atmosphere, unless otherwise ruled.

What about the house on the property? Is it real property or personal property? The rule is: If it's attached to the land (typically with a foundation in the ground), it's part of the land and thus part of the real estate and real property.

Insider's Tip

As you start looking at houses, remember that if something isn't permanently attached to the house (refrigerator, wall hangings), it is considered *personal property* and is *not* included in the sale unless specifically mentioned. (More on this topic in chapter 10.)

There are numerous ways that real property can be used. You can buy real estate to build a retail store, a wholesale warehouse, a factory, a rental apartment complex, or even a vacation home. In this book, we're covering residential real estate, the place where you will live most of the time. That can be a single-family residence (SFR) such as a house, a condominium (condo) apartment, a cooperative (co-op) apartment, or a Planned Unit Development (PUD).

What's the difference? How you own it! With a house, you own all rights to the land, residence, and other components yourself.

With a condo, you own the unit in which you live and share ownership of any common areas (entryway, yard, tennis courts, and the like). With a co-op, you own stock in a corporation that owns everything. When it comes to property rights, a PUD is like a house except that there's little or no space between units, and any common area is jointly owned; town houses are usually PUDs. More people buy houses than condos, co-ops, and town houses, but we'll cover buying all of them in this book.

Title and Other Rights

How does someone *know* who owns what real property rights? The owner is said to hold *title* to the property. This is very important to you, the buyer, so let's take a quick look at what it means.

Title is evidence of real property rights. Somewhere in a nearby government building, on paper or on a microfiche, is a signed and recorded document declaring who owns each piece of real property in its jurisdiction. They keep track of title—and especially who owes taxes!

Let me clarify that title and possession are different things. If they weren't, no one could rent property from the owner. The landlord holds title to a rental apartment, but the renters purchase the right of temporary possession. As you start looking at property for sale, you may consider houses that currently have renters in them, so understanding their rights is important to buying.

There are a couple of ways of looking at title. If you get a mortgage, you can say that the lender actually owns the property and lets the buyer live in it; or you can think of it as the buyer owning the property *subject to* the rights of the lender. Some states see things the first way; some states see them the second. As a result, state laws are built from one of these two viewpoints. If the lender is considered the owner, it's a title-theory state; if the buyer technically owns the property, it's a lien-theory state. It's an issue of law that leads to slight differences in how buyers take title in various states, though most states follow the lien theory. If you're selling a house in a lien-theory state and buying one in a title-theory state, you'll see some differences in the paperwork. Otherwise, the process is about the same.

So let's continue with ways buyers can take title to real property. Most buyers take absolute title to the property—called *fee absolute* or *fee simple. Fee* means ownership. The owners can do anything they want with the property as long as it doesn't violate zoning or other laws. (They can't turn a house into a factory, for example.)

> ## *Lingo*
>
> *Fee absolute* or *fee simple* means that the owner of the real property has absolute ownership, can sell or otherwise dispose of the property during his or her lifetime, and can will the rights of ownership to another upon the owner's demise.

An owner also can say that the property can only be used for a specific purpose, such as an owner who wills land to be a school. That's called *fee defeasible,* or voidable ownership. Most residential property *doesn't* have this type of title.

You also can hold title to property for as long as you live, with it transferred to someone else on your demise. That's called a *life estate.* Some retirement communities sell residences with this type of title. Once the occupants die, the title reverts to the corporation, which can then resell it. This makes sense for those who don't need to purchase absolute rights, because a life estate typically is cheaper.

As mentioned earlier, you can buy the right of possession without purchasing the right of ownership. If that right is for a specified period of time (one, five, twenty years), what you're getting is a *lease.* It gives you most of the rights of ownership, but only for the stated time. For example, if you're moving to another city for your job and know you will only be there for three years, you can get a three-year lease on a residence and enjoy whatever rights the owner sells you, including decorating and even remodeling to suit your tastes. You might even be required to pay property taxes and other assessments.

Pitfall

Make sure you know exactly what type of title you're getting when you buy real property. If something happens to you or you try to sell the property someday, you may find out that you have nothing to give. This is especially true of apartments (condos, co-ops). If there is *any* doubt in your mind, ask a real estate attorney or title insurance officer to explain what rights you're buying.

Here's one more thing to think about as you consider property rights. An *easement* is the right that someone else has to use your property for a specific purpose. Why would you ever consider such a thing? Because you want electrical, sewer, and water service! In order for these services to come onto your property, the utility companies must first ask your permission. If your title includes specific easements, however, they already have that right and don't have to ask. In fact, the easement was probably added to the title before a residence was built, so you may not have a choice in the matter. When you take title to the property, you accept any prior easements (though they can be changed with the help of an attorney). When you buy property, the title report will include specific information about easements to the property.

Out in front of your residence, the city or county probably has an easement over your property because, in many places, you actually own the property up to about the center of the road. Because title includes a road easement, though, you can't throw up a barricade some fine morning and start charging people to drive over your property. The owner has already agreed to let people pass over it. Conversely, other people are letting you drive over their property. That's an easement.

In addition, someone owns the rights to any and all minerals in your new property. It may be you or it may be someone else. If you find gold on your land, you may not be able to keep it. Chances are, however, that the gold, silver, oil, and just about everything else of great value was removed before the house was ever built; this is a nonissue in most locations. If you are concerned about mineral rights on the property you're buying, speak with an attorney or a title company officer to get an understanding of who owns what rights.

There's one other set of rights that impact residential property: riparian. These are rights you may have—or not have—regarding bodies of water on or adjacent to your property. Is it *your* water? Can you dump in it? Whom do you share these rights with? These are all property right and title questions that you may need answers to. Again, a title officer or attorney can explain them to you as they pertain to any property you buy.

Transferring Title

So now you know what title is all about. But how can you make sure that you are getting good and clear title to property you buy?

First and foremost, make sure that the person selling you the property rights has the right to do so! Fortunately, there are folks who make a living at researching and verifying titles on property: title companies. They use public records as well as their own extensive files on every property in your area to know who owns what rights. Most also will insure title to property, guaranteeing that they will pay for the defense of a property's title in court or even pay a judgment ordered by the court if the title isn't what they say it is. That's title insurance. You'll learn more about title insurance companies in the coming chapters.

As a buyer, there are various ways that you can *take title,* or own rights to a property. That's important because it indicates your ownership interest (by yourself, or with others) as well as what will happen to the property if an owner dies, called *right of survivorship*. If, for example, there is a divorce, how the owners hold title will be important. As a buyer, you want to know what title is being offered as well as how you want to hold it. When it's transferred, the way that title is held usually can be changed, so you will want to know your options.

Lingo

Tenancy is the right of possession of real estate, including the right of ownership and occupancy. There are various forms of tenancy as defined by state laws.

Let's take a quick look at how title can be held. It's a simplified description always subject to state laws, so you may hear slightly different terms. The intent, however, is about the same wherever you buy or sell title.

➤ *Tenancy by the entirety* gives husband and wife *equal right of possession* and the right of survivorship (if one dies, the other gets the property). This is sometimes called community property.

➤ *Joint tenancy* offers two or more people *undivided interest* in the property with the right of survivorship; it's similar to tenancy by the entirety.

➤ *Tenancy in common* gives two or more people undivided interest in the property but *no* right of survivorship (if one dies, the property must be sold).

There are other forms and other names for these forms, but their intent is to define who gets what rights, including the right to the property if one of the owners dies. When property title transfers to you, make sure you know what you're getting.

During the buying process, someone (agent, seller, escrow service, you) will request an *abstract of title* from a title company. It's a summary of the historical record of title for that specific piece of property, often dating back to when the parcel was part of a larger parcel that was subdivided. If you're using an agent, she or he may get this and review it for you, but, frankly, most don't.

Insider's Tip

Every piece of real estate in your area is defined, and title changes are recorded, at a city or county courthouse. It's public record so you can, at any time, go down and find out about property you're considering buying. It helps if you have the legal description, but even an address can get you basic information. Visit the local property tax office and the local planning office, too.

Once the abstract of title has been reviewed and okayed, the title company issues a *binder* or insurance policy on the title. If you're dealing with a lender, you'll need that binder to get the money to buy the house.

Escrow Basics

As you can see, there's a ton of paperwork involved in buying a house. There are agreements, title papers, loan papers, and lots of documents to help protect the sellers and agents. Everything must be pulled together for the closing transaction. And someone you all trust has to keep track of the title and money that's changing hands. Who does this?

An *escrow agent* is a trusted third party that works as a go-between for the seller, buyer, agent, lender, title company, and anyone else involved in a real estate transaction. The agent follows the instructions from the signed and countersigned purchase agreement—who gets what, when, and how—then takes care of all the paperwork, math, and transfers to make it happen.

An escrow agent can be independent or part of the lender's or title company's staff. When buying property, it's typically smarter to

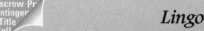

Lingo

Escrow is an agreement between two or more parties to allow a disinterested third party to manage a transaction following agreed-upon instructions.

Insider's Tip

If the purchase has some unusual terms or title issues, consider hiring a real estate attorney to perform the escrow function. This is an especially good idea if you've already found a trusted attorney who offers this service. It's more expensive than an escrow service, but can save you some headaches.

use an independent escrow company, though a title company is a qualified third party for most transactions. Lenders should only be used as escrow agents if you are refinancing your mortgage.

Chapters 11 and 18 will more thoroughly cover the closing of a real estate transaction, including requirements, who typically pays for what, and how not to get overcharged when you're most vulnerable.

Summary

You've learned more about real estate transactions in this chapter than *some* agents know. You've learned about property rights, what title is, how title can be taken, and how real estate transactions are closed. Along the way, I've given you some valuable tips to save time, trouble, and money. Whether you plan to use a real estate agent (part 2), have decided to buy property without an agent (part 3), or really don't know for sure quite yet, this introductory chapter and this part serve as a solid foundation for buying a house or apartment.

CHAPTER 2

It's a Buyer's Market

*Y*ou've probably heard the terms *buyer's market* and *seller's market*—meaning that one or the other has the upper hand in negotiating the best price. Let me tell you a trade secret: It's *always* a buyer's market! In this chapter, I'll tell you why this is true—and what you can do as a buyer to take advantage of this truth.

Lingo

A *seller's market* occurs when there is a greater demand for housing than the supply offers, giving sellers a perceived advantage in pricing and selling their property. A *buyer's market* occurs when buyers have a wide choice of properties because of local economic downturns or other factors.

The Marketplace

There are all types of marketplaces. There's the farmer's market where buyers and sellers congregate to exchange money for vegetables, sometimes haggling over prices until a deal is made. There's the supermarket where no-haggle prices are marked, take it or leave it. There's the stock market where the price is typically set by competition among buyers. What they all have in common is that sellers and buyers get together, estimate the value of something, and, if agreeable, exchange the thing for money.

How does the real estate market fall into this structure? There are sellers, buyers, the valuation, and the exchange of money and possession. It, too, is a marketplace just like the farmer's market, the supermarket, and the stock market, though it isn't in a specific location. The commodity—property rights—is different, but about everything else is the same whether you're selling and buying cantaloupes or condos. Of course, the prices are different; you wouldn't pay $200,000 for a cantaloupe no matter how delicious it was!

So who actually sets the price of property, the seller or the buyer? The market value of a specific piece of property is the price at which a willing seller and a willing buyer agree to exchange property title for money. But how do they know what the market value really is? If they don't buy and sell property every day (and most don't), how do the seller and buyer know if the price is "fair"?

The answer is that someone who knows more about the current real estate market than they do completes an appraisal of market value. An *appraisal* is an estimate of or opinion about the value of a specific piece of property. As an opinion, it is subject to elements beyond established facts. Maybe it's what the seller *wants* to sell the property for or the buyer *wants* to pay for it, but until they actually exchange title and money, it's not a fact; the asking price is an opinion.

So where does this opinion come from? It's probably based on the facts of what comparable properties in the area have recently sold for, as well as charts and tables in real estate appraisal books (covered in chapter 15). But *which* sales and *how* tables are interpreted are variables, making these numbers opinions. You can hire two professional appraisers with comparable credentials to do an appraisal on the same residence and get two different valuations! That's because appraisals are not facts, but opinions.

I'll share another secret: The same appraiser can produce appraisals with different valuations depending on who hired him or her. If the lender ordered the appraisal, it will probably be more conservative (as lenders are) in valuation than one ordered by the seller.

In addition, a real estate agent typically develops a *market analysis,* her or his estimate or opinion of the selling price of a residence. It's *not* an appraisal. It looks at recent sales of comparable properties but doesn't consider cost or replacement value, as a professional appraisal does. Because it is based on which properties are selected as comparables, it, too, is an opinion.

There's also something called a *tax appraisal* that a city or county taxing authority uses to defend property tax assessments. It's not *really* an analysis or appraisal of market value. I'll cover tax appraisals in chapter 15.

Insider's Tip

If the sale price of a residential property is disputed in court and the price is within about 5 percent of a professional appraisal ($10,000 on a $200,000 house), the dispute will probably be kicked out of court. The courts think that this margin of error is just too close to call because they recognize that valuation is an opinion, not a fact.

Back to the point that it's really a buyer's market. All markets are based on supply and demand. Because there is a relatively static amount of real property, I argue that it's up to the buyers to set the price, based on competition with other *buyers*. The seller really doesn't set the final price. If only one buyer comes forward to purchase a piece of property, it's that one buyer who controls the final price. If additional buyers come in and compete for the property, the price may go up, but it's because the buyers are competing. The seller *asks* for a specific price. It's the buyer who says yes or no, or offers a different price (usually lower, but sometimes higher than the seller asks, as you'll later see). The buyer always has the option of saying no and moving on to another seller *or* to another real estate marketplace. The seller cannot move the property to another marketplace. That's why it's really a buyer's marketplace. If sellers could fill up dump trucks with their property rights and move them to a better marketplace, it would be a true seller's market. Until then, it's a buyer's market.

The Buyer

So what does this mean for you, the buyer? It means you have more control over the final price and terms of a property purchase than you may have thought. Of course, you don't have *full* control—this is still a negotiated transfer of title and money—but you are in a good position to set price and terms. You always can move your money to a different marketplace. As noted, the seller can't.

Your exact bargaining position in the negotiating process depends on why you are buying property in the first place. Some must. Some want. Most buyers purchase property for both reasons. Let's discuss why *you* are considering buying and what it means toward getting what you want for a fair price.

Insider's Tip

Everything is negotiable—but not everything should be negotiated! Often, the purchase price of a home is less negotiable than other components of the transaction such as date of occupancy, who pays for what, and what personal property is included in the sale. If you feel that the asking price is equitable, consider what concessions to the terms would benefit you. You're more likely to get them than by trying to get a drop in the price.

The number one reason why people buy property is that they can. They've been renters because they prefer the flexibility or the reduced requirements on their time that renting offers—or they didn't have the down payment or credit rating together.

Maybe they aren't quite established in their career and need to be flexible to be employable. They want to join the two-thirds of all Americans who own the place where they live. Even if they know they may have to move on short notice, they understand that investing in residential real estate is better than giving the money to a landlord each month to invest in residential real estate.

Other buyers in the real estate marketplace are movin' on up. They've owned a home or two and now want to upgrade to one that offers more amenities: more room, better schools, closer to work or to play, prestige. Maybe they are moving from a marketplace where $200,000 will get them a fixer-upper to one that offers a mansion for the same money. If their income source is portable—and more are these days—they are in a better position to pick and choose the real estate marketplace in which they buy. Or they can consider homes in another marketplace as close as ten miles away.

Some buyers are simplifying either because they want to (fewer family members at home) or because they have to (job cuts). They are trading their future income and/or some property equity for a residence that better fits their needs and wants. It may be a single or couple ready to retire to a smaller residence in a warmer climate. Or it could be that the local job market has dried up and the family needs to move to a better one, simultaneously simplifying their home.

Insider's Tip

If you must move to a new area or marketplace to purchase a home, either do your homework about the local real estate marketplace or hire someone who can help you understand it quickly. The Internet offers many opportunities for learning about other places, but the telephone works well, too.

So why is the reason that you, the buyer, have for purchasing property important? Because it helps you define how to finance the move (chapter 3), your needs (chapter 4), and whether you use a real estate agent or not (parts 2 and 3). Because you are portable and property is not, you have the upper hand in buying real estate. Buyers have more options than sellers.

The Seller

So why is the seller selling? For some of the same reasons that buyers buy. Sellers may want to move up or down home-wise, trade in their equity for a better home elsewhere, trim their costs by trimming their assets, or split assets in a divorce.

It's a buyer's market also because sellers typically are more motivated to sell than buyers are to buy. The sellers are the ones with the big nonportable assets. If a job change, lifestyle change, divorce, or other factor pressures them to sell, they probably have time limitations. That gives another advantage to the buyer.

Of course, there are so-called hot markets where homes are sold nearly as fast as they come onto the market, giving the seller a distinct advantage. But this advantage actually occurs because the *buyers* are competing. Find ways to reduce the competition (as this book offers) and you can move toward a more level playing field. Knowing how *all* marketplaces work is your first step in winning in this marketplace.

One more point: Many of you buyers are also sellers. You must sell one property to buy another. By knowing both sides of this marketplace, you can learn to increase competition among buyers for your property and thus increase your profits.

How does the seller sell a home? Some sign an agreement with a real estate broker to market and sell the house for them. Others buy a FOR SALE BY OWNER (FSBO, pronounced "fizz-bo") sign at the hardware store and plant it in their front yard. In part 2, I'll show you how to profitably work with a real estate agent. Part 3 will guide you through buying from FSBOs. Neither of the two is an inherently *better* way to buy a home; they're just different ways. Your real estate agent is certainly not going to tell you how to buy from FSBOs, but many agents also don't make buying through an agent as easy as it should be. I'll tell you about dealing with both—as well as all the opportunities that even the smartest sellers or agents sometimes miss.

What does a FSBO need to sell her or his house? Guts! The seller can save a commission of more than $10,000 on the typical home by taking on all the headaches that a real estate agent is supposed to. Also, many FSBOs have learned from their experience that a poor agent is worse than no agent at all, so many say, *Why not?* And many aren't ready for the answer to that question: potential income loss, equity loss, lawsuits, marketing expenses, and grief. Uninformed sellers are eaten up by informed buyers every day.

Still, many FSBOs do quite well at selling their homes at an enhanced profit. In fact, an informed and motivated seller can typically do a better job than a mediocre real estate agent. The seller knows the property better and has only one client to please. If the seller discovers how to reach the widest group of potential buyers and knows a few things about marketing, a FSBO can be a smooth and mutually profitable transaction.

As a buyer, which do you want to work with, a dumb FSBO or a smart FSBO? The answer should be a smart one. An informed buyer may be able to gain an advantage over an uninformed seller, but the buyer will wind up doing most of the work. Lots of things can go wrong in such a relationship. I believe that the most profitable transactions are those with informed sellers and agents. This book is about informing you, the buyer.

How does a seller hire a real estate agent? The document that makes it all happen is called the *Residential Listing Agreement* or RLA, called by similar names in various states. Most offer the real estate broker and agents an exclusive authorization and right to sell a specific piece of property. The agreement includes a legal description of the property, terms of the sale (what's included, what isn't), the broker's and seller's duties, and *how the broker will be compensated.* In most states, this is a multiple-copy document of two or more pages. Lots of legalese, initials, and signatures. I'll give you some insights into opportunities this document offers the buyer in part 2.

Lingo

What's the difference between a real estate broker and an agent? A *broker* is a state-licensed real estate agent who, for a fee, acts on behalf of property owners or, in some cases, buyers. An *agent* is a state-licensed broker *or* salesperson. What are commonly called agents actually are real estate *salespeople* who work for and under the direction of a specific broker. There's more on the broker–agent relationship in chapter 5.

In essence, the RLA says that the named brokerage, its agents, and, if agreed, other brokers and agents (through a multiple listing service) may offer the specified property for sale in the marketplace. It also includes the property's list price and terms. Technically, the broker will not be paid the commission unless the offer brought from a buyer is *exactly* what is included in the RLA. Still, lower offers are commonly brought to sellers in purchase agreements and, if signed by the sellers, bind them to the new terms. That's good for the buyer to know, as you'll see in coming chapters.

Let's talk about another document that the seller fills out and signs, because it's nearly as important as the RLA. It's called by various names, typically the Real Estate Transfer Disclosure Statement (TDS), but most often known as the *disclosure statement* or *disclosure.* This paper documents what the seller knows about the property. In a way, it protects the broker against getting caught in a he-said/she-said argument between buyer and seller by putting things down on paper. It also helps buyers know more closely what they are getting.

The typical disclosure statement lists what items are on the property (though not necessarily included in a sale), such as utilities, structures, and appliances. It also asks sellers, point-blank, if they know of any defects in the property, residence, or title. Many disclosure statements also include an inspection sign-off by the agent and, eventually, by the buyer. It's a binding legal document intended to inform the buyer—and to protect the seller and agents in any disputes.

A real estate agent may not tell you about the disclosure statement because she or he is busy and forgot, because it will bring up some issues that the agent doesn't want to discuss, or because the agent didn't ask the seller to fill it out and sign it. Good agents will bring it up early in the buying process. Smart buyers will ask to see it as soon as they are interested in a specific property. In some states, the TDS is required and must be delivered to the buyer within a specified number of days of an offer to buy.

Insider's Tip

Want to see a listing agreement and disclosure statement? Professional agents who want informed buyers will sometimes share blank copies of these documents early in the buying process. It's just smart business to do so. Alternatively, you can purchase generic copies of these and other real estate forms through larger stationery stores.

The Players

One of the jobs an agent will do for you—or you will do for yourself if you're not using an agent—is interface with all the other experts in the real estate transaction process. You've already met real estate brokers and agents, above. Who are the other players?

Depending on your experience at buying and selling real estate, the trust you have in your agent or yourself to tackle legal issues, and the complexity of the transaction, you may want an attorney. Actually, you want a *real estate* attorney, someone who specializes in helping residential buyers and sellers through the legal aspects of transferring property title. Some can even handle the escrow closing for you. An attorney is an especially good investment if you are buying something you've not purchased before, such as a condominium, town house, or cooperative apartment. Also, many neighborhoods and developments will have covenants and restrictions that limit what you can do with your property. You should understand these limitations before buying—and your agent may not be able to help sort it all out. I'll cover hiring and using a good real estate attorney in chapter 12.

You'll probably need a lender to help buy your home. So one of the major players in your transaction will be that lender and all the folks in the lender's office. Chapter 3 will tell you more about how to understand, choose, and use the right lender. You'll also learn about mortgages and other types of financing in the next chapter.

Pitfall

Beware of under-the-table financing deals where sellers or others get or give money for concessions made outside the real estate transaction. Bluntly, these are finder's fees and kickbacks. First, they typically are not in writing, so they're not enforceable. More important, they're probably illegal.

Mentioned in chapter 1, the title company and the escrow company are both important players as you buy property. Because they need you as much as you need them, you should find them helpful and cooperative. Unfortunately, not all of them are as thorough as others. Even recommended experts should be checked out carefully before you hire them. Chapters 11 and 18 will tell you more about how to get professional service from them.

There are many other experts as well in the real estate market—professional consultants and service providers that help sellers sell and buyers buy without actually being in the middle of the transaction. They include appraisers, inspectors, advertisement publications, FSBO services, and financial advisers. You'll learn more about getting the most from each as we continue your profitable education in buying residential real estate.

Summary

As you've seen, real estate is *really* a buyer's market, and you have numerous options and opportunities as you ply the marketplace looking for what you want at a fair price. Knowing what motivates buyers and sellers, and understanding how agents can help or hinder the process, is a major step. You've also learned how price is established in the marketplace: It's set by *you,* the buyer.

CHAPTER 3

Lenders Hold the Keys

*W*ouldn't it be nice if lottery tickets were the primary source of home financing? Buy a hundred dollars in lottery tickets and you can buy the home of your dreams. In your dreams!

Instead, most of us have to save and scrimp until we have enough for the down payment on our first home, then use the profit from each home to get into the next one. We know that investing in residential property is about the best financial investment we can make, but it's still difficult to get the money together.

The good news is that just about *anybody* can borrow the money needed to buy a house. The bad news is that it may not be anywhere near the house you want, and the interest rate may be comparable to that of credit cards. Because some real estate agents are uncomfortable asking you about your financial condition, you may need to find out about financing on your own. That's not a bad thing, though, because educating yourself as to how lenders work can help you get lending terms that many agents can't.

So here's Home Financing 101.

The Money Market

Contrary to wishful thinking, money does not grow on trees. So where *does* it come from?

Money is a method of exchanging things of value. If you work in an office or factory for eight hours and the boss gives you some money, you've exchanged your labor for money that you can then exchange for food, rent/mortgage, video rentals, or whatever. If you make more than you spend, you can save some of this money, stuffing it in a box or taking it to a bank where it earns a little interest. The bank then loans out your money—and that from thousands of other savers—to folks buying a house based on their promise to pay it back. The bank lender keeps the difference between the interest that's paid to them by the borrower and what they have to pay to you, the saver.

Sounds simple enough. The money market is much more complex than that, but the above description covers the principles of lending. Over the years, layers of people and services have been added to give borrowers options—and to make things more profitable for lenders. There is a checks and balances system within lending, however, that tilts to your advantage. It's called competition! By knowing how the money market works and how to make it work, you can choose the lender with the best package *for you.* And chances are your real estate agent won't take the time needed to get you the best-best deal. You may be on your own.

Who are these lenders, anyway? Where can you apply for a loan to buy residential property? Here's the short list:

➤ Mortgage bankers

➤ Mortgage brokers

➤ Savings associations

➤ Savings banks

➤ Commercial banks

➤ Life insurance companies

➤ Pension funds

➤ Private investors

➤ The seller

Mortgage bankers and mortgage brokers are increasingly the most common sources of home loans. They typically don't have much money of their own. Instead, mortgage bankers borrow from banks, and mortgage brokers sell loans to banks and other financial resources. They are middlemen. By specializing in home loans rather than car and signature (no-collateral) loans, they can often get the lowest rates for you and still make a profit. I'll show you how to shop around and get the *best* rates in chapter 8.

Insider's Tip

What if you just can't get a lender interested in loaning you the money you need to buy a house or apartment? In some cases, you can turn to seller financing. You make payments directly to the seller instead of to a mortgage lender. You'll probably pay a higher interest rate, but some sellers prefer to take payments rather than a lump sum. Transaction costs may be lower than through a bank. Just make sure you get a real estate attorney to look over and explain the legal documents.

How Lenders Lend

Okay, saver, you now want to become a borrower to get a home. So let's consider the home-lending process. First, consider what you *as a lender* (after all, it's some of your savings that the lender is passing out) want to know about a potential borrower. You probably want to make sure the borrower:

➤ Has sufficient income to make the loan payments.

➤ Has income potential to make payments in the future.

➤ Has paid other bills when due (credit history).

➤ Has some other assets that can be tapped if needed.

➤ Is buying property that could be resold without much loss if somehow the borrower can't keep up payments.

➤ Can pay off the loan if the property is sold (due-on-sale clause).

You, as a saver, want to make sure that the lender considers these factors before offering your money to a potential borrower. Let's turn things around. You're now the borrower and the smart lender is asking these same questions of you. And the answers must be verifiable; the lender must have some way of making sure you, the borrower, are telling the truth. So the lender needs:

➤ Proof of income (check stubs, income tax statements).

➤ Verifiable employment history in a trade in which you have training and/or experience.

➤ A good credit report.

➤ A list of your assets (what you own) and liabilities (what you owe).

➤ An appraisal of the property's market value.

Because lenders must work with facts rather than opinions, they typically use a standardized loan application form, called a Uniform Residential Loan Application (URLA), that includes sections to indicate:

➤ Type of mortgage and terms of loan.

➤ Property information and purpose of loan.

➤ Borrower and co-borrower information (name, address).

➤ Employment information.

➤ Monthly income and housing expense information.

➤ Assets and liabilities.

➤ Transaction details.

➤ Declarations (bankruptcy, lawsuits, citizenship, and so on).

➤ Terms and signatures.

In fact, most lenders use a specific form developed by Fannie Mae and Freddie Mac, two institutions you'll learn more about later in this chapter. By standardizing the loan application, it's easier for lenders to verify and compare borrowers to determine who gets what loan and at what rate. Again, I'll show you how to get the best loan you can later in this chapter.

Mortgages

You've heard of mortgages, certainly, but may not be clear on exactly what they are and how to find the one you need. Don't feel bad—some real estate agents don't know enough about mortgages, either. They may pass you off to a friend in the mortgage business and hope you can work something out so you can buy a home from them. Most real estate agents are pros, but too many are not, and you should know what you're getting into. After all, it's *your* money!

Lingo

A *mortgage* is a legal document that creates a lien against real estate as security toward payment of a specified debt. A *lien* is the right the lender has to the property title. You can't sell the property title unless the lien is simultaneously paid off. Think of the mortgagor (one that loans) as a co-owner.

Let's review first and second mortgages. The primary loan that you get on a house is called the first mortgage. A subsequent loan (before the first one is paid off) is the second mortgage. If the property is sold, the holder of the first mortgage gets its money first, then the holder of any second mortgage gets paid, followed by you, the so-called owner. Second mortgages are often called remodeling loans because that's what many people use the money for.

Mortgages are also named by how the interest rate is established. A *fixed rate mortgage* has the same interest rate applied over the entire life of the mortgage (fifteen years, thirty years, what have you). An *adjustable rate mortgage* (ARM) will adjust the interest at least once during its life. How much it adjusts, when, and who says so are spelled out in the terms of the loan. The interest rate is based on a specific economic indicator called an *index*.

Lingo

A mortgage is intended to cover the difference between your down payment and the purchase price. The ratio of the mortgage to the purchase price is called the *loan-to-value* (LTV) ratio and is important to lenders. A $160,000 mortgage on a $200,000 residence is an 80 percent LTV. Any ratio higher than this (such as 90 percent LTV) requires *private mortgage insurance* (PMI), with the premium tacked onto your monthly payment of principal and interest (PI).

Insider's Tip

You're going to be hearing a lot about *Truth in Lending* as you finance a house—or at least you *should* be hearing about it. In plain English, it's a federal law that requires lenders to disclose terms and conditions in a manner that makes it easier for the consumer to compare apples to apples. It also intends to show you what the actual costs of lending will be. I'll tell you more as we get further into lending.

With ARMs, you are betting that the interest rate will go down or stay the same over its length or term. The lender typically doesn't care if the index goes up or down, because its profit is based on the difference between the index and the rate you pay—called the *margin, spread,* or *differential.* It's the lender's fee for originating the loan.

ARMs typically have caps as well. *Caps* are limits to how much the loan can go up or down. A mortgage can have a *periodic cap,* which states how much it can change over a specified period of the loan, or a *lifetime cap,* the amount it can change over the lifetime or term of the loan. It's typically a percent of interest, such as a 2 percent cap; a 6 percent ARM, for example, can't go over 8 percent—or below 4 percent.

So which type of loan is best for you? It depends on many factors, including the current fixed interest rate, the index being used, and how you think interest rates will change in the future. I'll show you how to get some good advice to help you with your decision, but it's one you are going to have to make. Your agent can't *and shouldn't* make this decision for you. Fortunately, it isn't forever. You can often renegotiate mortgage rates or even refinance in a few years if you get caught in an unsatisfactory mortgage.

Insider's Tip

Some lenders offer special mortgages with graduated payments, starting lower and increasing over a specified period until they are actually higher than a standard mortgage. For some borrowers, this is a good option, allowing them to qualify for a more valuable home than they could otherwise afford. It also can be a disaster, however, getting buyers into something they can't pay for. Be careful!

Fannie and Freddie

So who are Fannie and Freddie, and what do they have to do with your borrowing money to buy a house or apartment? They are two major reasons why the process of getting a mortgage is more streamlined than it used to be (though there's lots more paperwork today).

The Federal National Mortgage Association (FNMA or Fannie Mae) is a big stockholder corporation that buys mortgages from mortgage brokers and others. It buys *millions* of mortgages, spreading the risk around wider than a mortgage broker can do. You can meet Fannie Mae online at www.fanniemae.com.

The Federal Home Loan Mortgage Corporation (FHLMC or Freddie Mac) buys mortgages from savings associations. It, too, buys millions of them to spread the risk among investors. Freddie Mac is online at www.freddiemac.com.

The mortgage market is so standardized today (for efficiency and lower operating expenses) that Fannie and Freddie share the same loan application. The Uniform Residential Loan Application or URLA mentioned before is Fannie Mae Form 1003 and also Freddie Mac Form 65.

Fannie and Freddie are the big players in what's called the secondary mortgage market, responsible for more than half of all new mortgages. They keep the supply of money for housing widely available and at a lower cost through competition. Once a week, these institutions hold auctions, selling off groups of mortgages to the highest bidders. The bidders typically are security investors looking for a safe way to invest money—lots of money. Of course, *you* don't get a loan directly from Fannie or Freddie; your lender does. Your lender is selling your loan, though the lender may continue in the transaction by servicing the loan for a small fee.

Insider's Tip

There are numerous government programs that offer special mortgages and mortgage rates to veterans, low-income buyers, first-home buyers, and others. I'll tell you more about them in chapters 8 and 16.

The reason for the standardized loan apps and verifications is to make mortgages more homogeneous and less risky for investors. Less risk means lower interest rates. Fannie and Freddie are conduits between investors and borrowers, taking a small profit for their efficiency.

Of course, there are other players in the secondary mortgage market as well as other ways of getting a mortgage, but chances are the mortgage you get will be through this channel. Knowing how it works can help you as a consumer.

Insider's Tip

Mortgages are referred to as conforming and nonconforming. A *conforming* loan is one that is eligible for purchase by Fannie Mae or Freddie Mac. It conforms to their guidelines. The loan limit for conforming mortgages in 2004 is $333,700, and it is adjusted upward every year. A *nonconforming* loan is above that and typically subject to slightly higher interest rates.

Summary

Yes, lenders probably *do* hold the keys to your next home. Still, *you* hold the keys to getting the best deal from lenders. You understand how the money market works, how lenders lend, how mortgages are structured, and how they are sold in the secondary mortgage market. Equally important, you know how lenders rate you as well as how to improve your rating so that you get the mortgage you want at the lowest cost. *You* are in charge!

CHAPTER 4

Getting the Home You *Really* Want

*T*he agent says, "Sure, I think we have a house in that price range. Let's go see if it's still standing!"

If you're buying your first home, your twelfth home, or your first home in a new marketplace, you're probably going to face sticker shock. It's the moment right after the real estate agent shows you the home you want and tells you the asking price. The symptoms of sticker shock are a drop in the jaw and a catch in the throat. It's the point where you either say, "I'll stay where I am," or, "I wonder if Uncle Herbert can help us here?"

The third option is to take inventory of what you *really* want and learn more about how to get it—things your real estate agent may not tell you. You can invest an hour of your time and save thousands of dollars and years of grief due to buying a home you really don't want. Let's get started.

Determining Your Needs and Wants

You're really not buying a house, condo, co-op, or town house, of course. You're looking for a *home*. A home is where you *live*. It's more than just rooms and plumbing. It's furniture, a neighborhood, proximity, safety, conveniences, status, and more. It's also something you can afford. You can't make it a home if you have to move out once the huge mortgage is due.

So the first step toward getting the home you really want is determining what your needs and wants are. A *need* is a requirement; a *want* is a desire. You may need a job, but you want one that has certain benefits. You need a house that is safe and secure; you want one that has specific amenities. You don't want to move into a nice home in a neighborhood where you don't feel safe. You want a fancy house, but you need one that fits in your budget.

In addition, you must consider what the others in your living group need and want, balancing them with the need to keep the home affordable. A daughter may need special education. A son may want to continue playing on the same high school football team. A husband or wife may want to live near a college to return to school soon. A living partner may need proximity to a long-term job. It's all about compromises.

Because selecting a home is a decision with long-term repercussions, I suggest that you take some time to develop a five-year plan for you and your living group, based on everyone's input. In this world of drive-up fast food, it's difficult to plan that far ahead, but remember that the plan is written on paper, not stone. It's your best guess. It may even seem like a waste of time, but, as the philosophers say, if you don't know where you're going how will you know when you get there? So try to picture what you'd realistically like your life to be like in five years and ask the same of living group members who understand the concept.

Sure, most of this is commonsense stuff. But few people actually make a five-year plan and consider it when buying a home. It's not that difficult to do, and the advantages certainly outweigh the time needed to do it. It's just that it's not easy for most people to be so introspective and develop a forecast. My advice: Do it anyway.

Studying the Marketplace

Buying real estate is about educating yourself and, if needed, hiring educated advisers. One of the advantages that a good agent can offer is knowledge of specific neighborhoods in the community where you need or want to purchase a home. Unfortunately, the agent's knowledge may not be accurate, current, or objective. That means you need to find a trusted agent (chapter 6) or do your own homework (chapter 15). Even if you do hire an agent, you should verify any information you learn about specific neighborhoods.

Insider's Tip

As you start considering your next home, remember that one of the largest monthly bills you'll have—right after the mortgage payment—is the utility bill. In some areas of the country, the utility bill can exceed the mortgage payment during hot or cold months. So it makes sense to look for an energy-efficient high-tech home and appliances that can cut overall housing costs. Energy savings can help you get into the home you want.

What is a neighborhood? A *neighborhood* is an area of similar or compatible land uses. A large complex of condos is a neighborhood. If the adjoining residential structures are also condos of approximately the same value, they, too, are part of the neighborhood. If the adjoining area is made up of residential houses, commercial structures, or a trailer park, it is a separate neighborhood. A residential neighborhood can contain supporting commercial structures (grocery store, gas station, et cetera), but the function must primarily be residential. A large residential area may include numerous neighborhoods, each occupied primarily by people of similar incomes, lifestyles, and residential requirements. There are typically exceptions within a neighborhood, but most homes are comparable.

Finding a neighborhood in which you feel safe and that fits your financial and living requirements is important. Not only will your decision affect day-to-day life over the next few years, but it will also impact how easily and profitably you can sell your home if and when the time comes to do so.

So how can you find one or more neighborhoods that fit your requirements? First, buy a map of the area around where you work or plan to work. Then ask agents, lenders, friends, co-workers, and other respected advisers to help you identify and describe the primary neighborhoods in your area. If you already live in the area in which you are buying, you may already know something about many of the neighborhoods. If you're retiring to the Sun Belt, on the other hand, you may need to make a few visits before settling on specific cities, towns, and neighborhoods that fit your five-year plan.

Include on this map the location of your living group's jobs, schools (for the next five years), required services, and shopping. Then mark on it the major routes through the city, town, community, and neighborhoods. Not only do you want to get somewhere fast, you *don't* want others cutting through your neighborhood to do so. Investing a little time in mapping neighborhoods can save you many thousands of dollars and possibly years living somewhere that doesn't fit your *real* needs and wants.

Insider's Tip

Larger daily newspapers often include home ads identified by neighborhood. Study the Friday or Sunday paper ads for structure, asking advisers where these neighborhoods are. You also may be able to tell what price ranges are by comparing the typical price for a three-bedroom, two-bath home in each of the neighborhood's ads. The ads also may give you clues to neighborhood amenities.

Next, start a Buyer's Notebook. It can be a bound book with lined pages, a spiral notebook, or some other method of keeping track of lists and facts. If you're into personal digital (or data) assistants (PDAs) or are ready to start, consider using it as your Buyer's Notebook, storing needs lists, preferences, agent and lender contact information, and whatever else you need to track. Having a single location for all the info you're going to analyze will make the job much easier. You can even store maps on some PDAs.

Looking at Neighborhoods

Okay, you now have an idea of what neighborhoods you think may fit your long-term goals. Don't stop learning, though. As you begin looking at homes, you may quickly determine that what you've heard isn't what you see. Or you may identify nearby or on-the-way neighborhoods that better reflect your needs and wants. Keep an open mind and good notes.

Whether you use a real estate agent or not, it's really *your* responsibility to make sure you buy the home *you* want. Don't expect the experts to do this for you. If you've learned to trust the agent's opinion, you may not have to spend much time verifying it, but if you are getting conflicting information or none at all, you will need to do some of your own homework. Fortunately, it can be fun—though a little time-consuming. Here are some ideas:

➤ Drive through neighborhoods that seem to fit your housing needs, looking for real estate signs, traffic patterns, and other signs of life.

➤ If you come upon friendly walkers or yard workers, approach them with a smile and ask about the neighborhood.

➤ Get out of the car and listen for dogs, traffic, industrial noises, aircraft, emergency vehicles, and any other sounds that may affect your lifestyle.

➤ Take a look at the vehicles that populate the neighborhood, identifying typical age and condition as well as where they are parked (street, driveway, garage).

➤ If you can, return to preferred neighborhoods at various times of the day and night to determine commuter traffic patterns, the location of barking dogs, and the condition of streetlights.

I'll offer additional tips on looking at neighborhoods, streets, home groups, and individual properties in chapter 9. For now, identifying potential neighborhoods that meet your requirements is a big step toward finding the home you want.

Learning What You *Don't* Want

The main problem with shopping for a house or apartment is that there are just too many choices. If there were three home plans, all you'd have to do is select the best from the three. That's relatively easy. You'll probably have hundreds of potential properties to look at, however, depending on your needs, wants, and financial wherewithal. So how can you narrow the field a bit?

Of course, your needs-and-wants list, mortgage ability, and your neighborhood maps will reduce the options from which you have to choose. If you're looking for a four-bedroom home in Brightwood, for example, you can immediately scratch off two-bedroom homes in Hooverville. Or maybe you decide you don't want to consider homes that are less than fifteen hundred square feet in size. That's the process of elimination at work. As you contact FSBOs, drive by addresses your agent gives you, and take a look at homes for sale in your chosen neighborhoods, you'll compare each to your list and map. You'll try to determine how the property matches what you think you want. That's good.

Lingo

A *square foot* is an area one foot wide by one foot deep. Structures typically are measured by the square foot. Information on a house or apartment for sale includes the size in square feet. Square footages of rooms are indicated by the interior measurements: A ten-foot by ten-foot room is one hundred square feet (s.f.). Houses, apartments, and other groups of rooms are often indicated by the exterior measurements because it is easier.

You're also learning what you *don't* want. As you get into the home-shopping process, you may discover that you want a family room, but you *don't* want one that was converted from a garage. Or you *don't* want any home on a street that carries more than ten cars an hour. Or you *don't* want a home next to a school or retail business. You get the point. These are things you may not have considered when you made your list, but they become obvious as you begin looking at actual three-dimensional properties in real locations. Jot them down in your Buyer's Notebook.

Actually, many people shop this way. When buying a car, they circle interesting newspaper ads, then call to find out why they *don't* want that specific car: too many miles, wrong color, non-negotiable price, possible damage. They then go see the cars that pass the first test, trying to eliminate some more until they are left with one that passes the elimination test. That's the one. Although emotion is one of the considerations, a good-looking car with a bad engine is a bad car. It's the same with homes. Buy based on needs and wants—not emotions.

Pitfall

"I love this house! We can turn the utility room into a third bed-room, can't we?" Too many people buy homes based primarily on emotion, later learning why it's not the best way. Unfortunately, some unscrupulous agents and sellers sell primarily on emotion. "Sure, the utility room will make a great bedroom!" Beware any so-called experts who sell emotions rather than needs and wants.

Making Decisions You Can Live With

Buying a home is obviously a big decision that affects many aspects of your life and those of your living group. No pressure here! ☺ Fortunately, by using commonsense logic and communication, you can make sure you buy the right home at a fair price whether you use an agent or do it yourself. The real key is knowing what you want and what you can afford without selling the kids. So here are some valuable tips for making the best decision you can when buying your next home.

In many cases, the worst decision you can make is none at all. Especially in areas of high rent where homes are quickly appreciating in value, you may be getting behind financially by *not* buying. The longer you wait, the farther behind you will get. So, in this type of market, don't hold off because you're looking for the perfect house. It doesn't exist. Instead, buy a house, condo, co-op, or town house that meets many of your primary needs and wants. It will serve your housing requirement while teaching you what you want—and *don't* want—in your next home.

In some situations, however, it's actually better to rent for a while than to quickly buy. For example, if you're transferred to a new job or must move to a new location without the opportunity to do some research, getting a rental for a few months can give you the breathing room you need to make a better housing decision. You may rent a furnished place and put your stuff in storage, or you can mark the things you move as STORAGE and OPEN ME NOW.

Many folks need to first sell their existing home before buying a new one. If at all possible, do so. Whatever you do, stay off a "train"—a line of sellers and buyers each waiting on another sale so they can proceed with their transaction. Trains crash!

Insider's Tip

Few people can afford two homes without some type of offsetting income. One way to avoid this is to rent or lease your current home to a good tenant so that payments are offset by income, making qualifying for a mortgage on your new home easier. Ask lenders how to show the rental income on your loan application for the greatest chance of approval.

Summary

Getting the home you really want means first determining *what* you want: size, location, price, amenities, and so forth. Then you study the marketplace, select the neighborhoods that offer what you want, figure out what you *don't* want, and make decisions you can live with. It's really not rocket science, and many millions of people do this every year. By using commonsense logic and keeping emotions in their proper place, you can buy a home that will make future days easier.

PART TWO

Getting the Most from a Real Estate Agent

CHAPTER 5

How Agents Are *Supposed* to Work for You

*D*o you really *need* a real estate agent to buy a house or apartment? An agent may, for selfish reasons, tell you yes, but the real answer is no! You can legally buy and sell residential real estate *without* an agent. Thousands of people do it successfully every year. Part 3 of this book will show you how!

So the next question is: *Should* you use an agent to buy a home? That one's not as easy to answer; it depends on many factors, requirements, conditions, and your comfort level. To help you decide whether you need an agent in the first place, this chapter gives you a behind-the-scenes look at how agents are *supposed* to work. You'll learn how good agents earn their fee—and how much they get. The next chapter will help you find one of these good agents.

Understanding Agency

It's a fact that about 85 percent of all home sales in the United States each year involve real estate agents. That's millions of transactions that are helped along—or hindered—by licensed agents. What is it that these folks really do? Who hires them? For whom do they work? How do they get paid? What is their legal responsibility? These are all good questions that will be answered in this chapter.

As you learned in chapter 2, a real estate *agent* is a state-licensed broker or salesperson. What does that really mean? *Agency* is a legal term. It covers the relationship between a client (principal) and an agent, someone who is legally authorized to do something on behalf of the client for a fee. In the case of real estate, the client authorizes the agent to sell or buy real property for a fee. In most cases, the agreement authorizes the agent to hire subagents as well.

Lingo

What's the difference between a real estate agent and a Realtor? Anyone who passes the state real estate examination and pays the fees can use the title *real estate agent* or *real estate salesperson,* depending on state laws. A Realtor is a licensed agent who also is a member of the National Association of Realtors (NAR).

As you can imagine, whoever hires the agent is the one that gets the agent's allegiance. In fact, the agent has a *fiduciary* or legal obligation to work for the client and not for anyone else who may have an interest in the transaction.

So who actually hires the agent? In most transactions, who pays the agent's fees? If hired, to whom does the real estate agent owe a legal obligation to work for? *The seller!*

It may seem as if an agent is working for you, the buyer, but unless you actually hire that agent and agree to pay a fee, the agent is authorized and required to work for the seller's interest, not necessarily yours. Sure, the seller can't pay the fee unless there is a buyer—you—but the agent's legal obligation is to work on the seller's behalf.

By law, a real estate agent is *supposed* to tell you this—and good ones make it very clear because they don't want anyone suing them for misrepresentation. In fact, many state laws require that the seller, buyer, and agents all sign a document called an *agency disclosure.* But don't be fooled. The agency disclosure only tells you what agency options are available to the seller and buyer. The so-called disclosure doesn't really disclose what the relationship is for a specific transaction. Who is working for (and is paid by) whom is disclosed in other documents I'll discuss later.

Whom can the agent work for?

➤ A seller's agent works for the best interests of the seller.

➤ A buyer's agent works for the best interests of the buyer.

➤ A dual agent works for the best interests of both the seller and the buyer.

So why are most agency relationships with the seller rather than the buyer, or with both? Because, as covered in chapter 2, it's the seller who has the greatest need. The seller has this property that needs to be sold, so hires an agent. The agreement to sell, called the *listing*, engages the agent to work for the seller by bringing a qualified buyer.

Does this mean that you, the buyer, should hire a buyer's agent? Not necessarily. By being a smart consumer, you can take advantage of the legal role of the seller's agent to protect yourself. I'll show you how to use this relationship to your advantage in the next chapter.

Insider's Tip

In most residential real estate transactions, the agent is hired by and represents the seller. Many agents, however, prefer to specialize in one side of the home-buying process over the other. Some agents prefer to list homes, while others prefer to work with buyers. Find one who works better *with* buyers—but remember that she or he probably works *for* the seller.

Brokers and Agents

There sure seem to be a lot of salespeople in the real estate process: brokers, seller agents, buyer agents, salespeople, other sales offices. Who are they and how do they all work together?

As introduced in chapter 2, a real estate agent can be a broker or a salesperson. A broker is a licensed agent. All real estate transactions with an agent require a designated broker who is ultimately responsible for following the laws of agency in the transaction. The broker can hire one or more salespeople as well as other agents, called subagents. So a typical home sale can include:

> ➤ Listing broker (agent)

>> ➤ Listing salesperson(s)

> ➤ Selling broker (subagent)

>> ➤ Selling salesperson(s)

Because you are the buyer, the one with the money, you ultimately will be the one who indirectly (through the seller) pays all these people. Knowing how they get paid—and how much— can help you get your money's worth. The agents probably won't tell you what they are paid, so I will.

In a typical real estate transaction begun by the seller hiring a seller's agent, the commission is 5 to 7 percent for residential property (vacant land is usually 10 percent). Six percent is usual in most real estate markets. That's $12,000 of commission on a $200,000 house or apartment. Who gets what? In the same typical transaction, the listing agent (seller's agent) gets half ($6,000) and the selling agent (seller's agent working *with* the buyer) gets half ($6,000).

How much do the salespeople get? That depends on the employment agreement with their broker. Newer, less experienced agents typically get half of whatever their broker gets; that's $3,000 for selling a $200,000 home. More experienced salespeople with a good sales record may get 65, 75, or even 85 percent of what the broker gets ($3,900, $4,500, or $5,100). In many offices, the percentage goes up as total sales go up.

The salesperson doesn't get to keep all the money the broker pays. In some offices, the salesperson must rent a desk, pay franchise fees (such as those to Century 21 or Better Homes and Gardens Real Estate), pay some or all advertising fees, pay transaction (errors and omissions) insurance, and probably chip in for the coffee fund. In fact, a newer agent may be making minimum wage or less until skills and contacts are built. It's not the easiest way to make a living! Chapter 6 will show you how to hire the best of the best agents.

Lingo

A real estate *associate* can be a salesperson or a broker who works for another broker, depending on state laws.

Let me make another important point here: Real estate agency commissions are, by law, negotiable. If they weren't, the agencies could be charged with price-fixing, a federal offense. So most agencies allow, but discourage, the seller to negotiate the total commission paid on a property. It can be a percentage, a flat fee, or two thousand chickens. It's negotiable between the seller and the seller's agent.

As noted, the fee split between the brokers and their salespeople is negotiable based on the employment contract. What you may not know is that the listing broker or agent doesn't have to split the commission evenly with the selling broker. It can be 50–50, 60–40, or any other commission split the listing broker thinks will make a profitable sale for the office. If there is an abundance of buyers and few sellers, the listing agent can offer a smaller portion to the broker who brings the buyer. Or the listing broker can ask the seller for the right to sell the property only through the broker's office, an office exclusive.

Insider's Tip

Why do you, the buyer, care what split the listing agent offers the agent who brings the buyer? Because your agent may not be as inclined to show you properties that pay a lower commission!

One more point: The seller's agent is probably authorized to offer the property to subagents. Who are subagents? They include whoever brings the buyer into the transaction. But the term also covers any other real estate office with which the broker has a mutual agreement. This typically means members of a local real estate association and/or multiple listing service. All the member offices agree to share listings with other member offices, giving each agent access to many times more homes for sale than those his or her office has under contract. Alternatively, agents can negotiate individual "show and sell" deals with unaffiliated offices. That's good for you, the buyer.

Comparative Market Analysis

What exactly does the real estate agent offer to do for the seller? The agent brings the seller a qualified buyer (that's you!) who will purchase the home or apartment at a specified price. The seller doesn't have to sell unless the asking price and terms are met, although most sellers will look at offers lower than the asking price.

Where does the asking price come from? It could be some number that sellers think they want. More often it is based on a Comparative Market Analysis (CMA) developed by the real estate agent at no charge. It's usually based on the asking (not actual) price of comparable houses. It is an *opinion* of value.

Pitfall

Beware any agent who calls the CMA an appraisal. An appraisal is developed using sale prices as well as appraisal books, typically by a licensed appraiser charging $300 or more. Many agents use listing prices (how much the seller wants) rather than sale prices (how much the seller got) in their analysis. The test: Your lender will accept an appraisal but not a CMA as property valuation.

As a buyer, can you see a copy of the seller's CMA? No, you can't—unless the seller authorizes agents to show it to potential buyers. You can, however, request that your agent give you a list of comparables to a specific property to determine probable value. In coming chapters, I'll show you how to get it.

Seller's Listing

The Residential Listing Agreement (RLA) is a contract between the seller and a licensed real estate agent offering that agent (and his or her assigns) the right to sell a specific property under specific terms. The typical listing agreement is two to three pages long, spelling out:

➤ A legal description of the property.

➤ The terms of the sale (asking price, what's included, what's not).

➤ How the broker will be compensated.

➤ Who else is authorized to sell the property (subagents such as a multiple listing service).

➤ That the seller actually owns the property.

➤ What the broker can and cannot do in representing the property.

➤ How any disputes between the seller and agent will be resolved.

➤ The duration of the listing (important to a buyer).

➤ Whether the listing will be office-exclusive or put into the multiple listing service.

➤ Signatures (of course!).

There are many other elements to an RLA, specifying the relationship between the seller and agent. Most are intended to protect the agent.

Pitfall

Some real estate agents have "pocket listings," or properties that sellers have said they will sell if the right buyer comes along. Legally, there is no formal listing agreement, so the agent cannot represent the property as for sale. Be cautious.

At the same time the listing is signed, most agents also get the seller to complete—or at least start filling out—the seller's disclosure statement mentioned in chapter 2. The disclosure is intended to tell you, the buyer, what the seller knows about the property for sale. Its primary purpose, however, is to cover the agent against claims of misrepresentation: "The seller never told us about the leaky roof." Chances are you won't get to see a copy of the listing agreement, but you *will* see the disclosure statement—even if you have to ask for it.

Most RLAs are an "exclusive authorization and right to sell," meaning that if the agent or anyone authorized by the agent is instrumental in selling the property, the seller must pay a commission. Be aware that there are also "nonexclusive" (also known as "open") listings. This means the seller authorizes the listing agent to sell, but others can sell the property as well. A seller can sign only *one* exclusive, but can sign nonexclusives with every real estate broker in town. This isn't done frequently, except by home builders (chapter 14) and with some commercial properties.

More often, property owners who want to try selling on their own *and* using a real estate agent can sign an exclusive agency agreement with an agent and exclude paying commission to the agent if the seller makes the deal. These agreements can get a little sticky, and (for obvious reasons) most agents discourage them, so don't expect to see one. A real estate agent certainly isn't going to tell you that he or she doesn't have an exclusive listing!

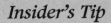

Insider's Tip

Knowing how long a property has been on the market gives you an advantage in negotiating. Agents may not (or may not be able to) tell you the age of a listing, but you can often find it in some paperwork about the property. Most city and suburban residential listings are for 90 days, rural homes are for 180 days, and vacant land typically is listed for six to twelve months. Once a listing has expired, the property can be relisted, so the home you're considering may have been on the market longer than it appears. Ask and look!

Typically if you look at a home with an agent or subagent but buy it directly from the seller after the listing expires, the agent has a right to collect a commission from the seller. Of course, that's the *seller's* problem, not yours.

Marketing the Listing

What is it that the listing agent does? Once the listing agreement is signed, the agent *should* begin a concerted marketing effort to get a qualified buyer for the property. That means having office showings (everyone in the office visits), putting the house on tour for all affiliated offices, scheduling open houses, putting an ad in the local newspapers and real estate publications, and calling up any potential buyers the agent is working with.

Unfortunately, some real estate agents "sit on the listing." That is, they do the math and determine that, in their real estate marketplace, two-thirds of the listings will sell within ninety days. So rather than spend time and money on marketing, they let other agents do all the work and know that, chances are, they will have a payday soon. Instead, they go get more listings, go play golf, or do anything except what they signed an agreement to do: market the seller's property.

On the other side of professionalism, there are agents who use a new listing to start working the phones, calling up prospective buyers to describe the property and offer to show it. They, as agents or subagents, may have already interviewed the sellers to determine things about the property that don't come across in the listing agreement and disclosure. They know that the fastest way to sell a listing (and get a commission) is to know what the sellers are selling, what buyers want, and match them up. That's the kind of agent you'll find in chapter 6!

Helping with Financing

Smart agents also know that matching up a seller and a buyer is only part of their job. In order to get the home or apartment sold, they must help the buyer find appropriate financing. They know, as you do (chapter 3), that the lenders hold the keys! They introduce potential buyers to various lenders, help buyers get prequalified, and even offer some creative financing options (seller financing, exchanges, unconventional financing, and the like) as needed.

Pitfall

Do real estate agents get kickbacks for making referrals to specific lenders? They'd better not! The Real Estate Settlement Procedures Act (RESPA) prohibits it.

In chapter 8, I'll show you how smart agents can help you get the money you need to buy the right home. In the next chapter, you'll learn how to find the best agent for your needs.

Summary

Real estate agents are *supposed* to work for the seller by helping qualified buyers purchase a house, condo, co-op, or town house that is appropriate to their needs and abilities. They are supposed to follow the laws of agency, cooperate with other professionals, efficiently market property listings, and answer financing and other questions that buyers have. They typically are paid by the seller, but you can help sellers get their money's worth by making agents work hard for you, the buyer.

CHAPTER 6

Selecting a Gem from Among the Duds

*T*he *right* real estate agent can make home buying easier, less time-consuming, and (very important) less expensive. The *wrong* agent can waste your time, your money, and your patience. So it's obviously important for you to find the right agent for you.

How? Actually, it's not that difficult to find good agents. There are telltale signs. And as with most relationships, there is no one *perfect* agent, but there are a few gems that really shine. That makes them easier to spot! In this chapter, I'll show you how to hire a real estate agent who will efficiently find the home that fits your requirements.

Insider's Tip

Why not just find a property that sounds good, call up the office, and ask the agent at the desk to show it to you? That's how many real estate relationships get started. The problem is that the listing may be nothing like the ad—and the agent may not be the best one in the office for you. Instead, follow my advice in this chapter to find the best agent who will find you the best property.

Gathering Duds

First, let's take a look at the duds. Real estate, like so many things, seems to follow the 80–20 rule: 80 percent of the business is done by 20 percent of the agents. The other 20 percent of the business is shared among the other 80 percent of the agents. So identifying the top 20 percent of all local agents will quickly narrow down the options.

Who are these duds, and what keeps them in the business? Many are part-time agents and part-time something else. Whatever else they are doing, they aren't fully dedicated to real estate, so why should you hire them? The first slow real estate market that comes along will force them into another part-time job. Until then, they will pick up a deal here and there to pay for gas and office expenses, but they won't be named top salesperson for the month.

Insider's Tip

What did agents do before they became top salespeople? Many have a background in sales or marketing. Some are from the construction industry. Others are from other walks of life. One great agent I know had previously been a landscaper. Another had worked as a painter in a truck factory. More important is what they have done *lately*.

It's not that some of them aren't nice people. They probably are. It's that they haven't, for whatever reason, made a commitment to putting their best efforts into helping others buy and sell real estate. A top agent lives and breathes real estate. Lesser agents may not see the newest listings. They may not hear about a new lender that's offering better mortgage terms. They're not available when you need them. They don't yet understand the value of service.

Of course, not all full-time agents should automatically go to your A-list. Some sell lots of homes because they are pushy, intimidating weaker buyers into transactions that they may later regret, or they work better with sellers and really don't have much experience helping buyers. They try to sell you something instead of helping you buy what you need.

Pitfall

Beware cherry-pickers—part-time agents who really are real estate investors looking for opportunities to profit from the mistakes and problems of others. Their *real* client is themselves, not you.

Insider's Tip

Do you want a salesperson who is *hard-sell* or *soft-sell?* Soft-sell is preferred, but the best agents are those who *don't* sell—they use their knowledge and skills to *help you buy*. These are the best agents for buyers.

So the field of potential real estate agents is quickly narrowing down. You want full-time agents who know how to help you buy real estate that fits your requirements. How can you cull them from the duds?

Culling

The *right* agent:

> ➤ Is a full-time licensed professional real estate agent with additional training.

> ➤ Has been active in real estate for at least one year, but preferably five or more.

> ➤ Works in an active real estate office that markets itself, its salespeople, and its properties.

> ➤ Is recommended by friends and other professionals.

> ➤ Has won numerous sales awards.

> ➤ Is obviously organized and efficient.

> ➤ Is always busy but never too busy to help.

➤ Is an outstanding communicator.

➤ Will tell you the truth about a property or transaction even if it means a lost sale.

Sound about right? Wouldn't you just *love* to find this agent and hire her or him to work for you? You can! Here are some insider's tips:

➤ Check newspaper classifieds and local real estate publications to identify the most active real estate offices that sell properties in the neighborhoods you've selected.

➤ Read the ads over a week or a month to determine who the top salespeople or listing agents are.

➤ If there is a weekly newspaper column about the local real estate market, read it for clues on the top agents for *buyers*.

➤ Call the various offices asking for information about a specific listing to determine how professionally the salespeople handle your questions. Smart agents will carefully get as much information from you as you from them.

➤ Visit the selected offices, telling staff that you're waiting for someone (they'll probably leave you alone), then look around for sales awards on the wall above specific agents' desks.

➤ Watch office activity for a few minutes to determine if there are support staff to help agents with office functions.

➤ Without being obvious, listen to office conversations, because they often reflect management's attitude: helpful, courteous, grudging, superior, dishonest, cautious, or bored.

➤ Make notes on your impressions and continue visiting other offices. The entire process may only take a couple of hours and can save you many days of wasted time with agents who don't fit your requirements.

➤ Visit the local title company, mortgage brokers, banks, and the like, and ask if they can recommend a local real estate agent who works well with buyers.

➤ Ask your friends or co-workers for a recommendation.

Selecting the Best

Once you've narrowed down your search to a few of the leading real estate offices, you can select and interview the best salespeople from those offices. Why not select the salesperson first, accepting the office that the person works for? That's okay, too, except that you're actually "hiring" a brokerage, not just an individual salesperson. You'll use the services of support staff and even other agents in the office as you find and buy your home. It's smarter to pick the office first, knowing that the area's better salespeople have probably been hired by that office.

Here's what I suggest you do next: Interview the brokers. As covered in chapter 5, it's the broker who is ultimately responsible for all real estate transactions that go through the office. You want to make sure that they will be handled professionally. Good bosses typically hire good people. As a smart buyer, you want to hire good bosses.

What will you ask the brokers?

➤ *What is your training and experience in marketing real estate?*

➤ *Tell me when and why you started this office?*

➤ If they are at a franchise office: *Why did you choose XYZ franchise?*

➤ *How successful has your office been helping buyers?* You're looking for verifiable statistics such as the number of homes they sold last year, how many of these were their own listings, and how many were listed by other offices.

➤ *Who are the two salespeople in your office most successful at helping buyers with my particular needs?*

➤ *Will you introduce me to them?* Being introduced to buyers by the broker makes salespeople work a little harder.

What will you ask the salespeople?

➤ *How do you typically help buyers find the right home for them?*

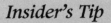

Insider's Tip

Real estate franchises are like any other franchises: They bring a brand name and proven process to local real estate offices. Many franchises are national, others regional, and some are local. In each case, ownership of the office is local. You are hiring the local broker, not the franchise.

➤ *What is your typical workweek—days, hours, on-call?* Make sure this schedule matches the times when you prefer to look at properties.

➤ *Do you preview the new properties listed?*

➤ *Do you have an assistant or another agent who will provide help if you are unavailable?*

➤ *How do you help buyers get financing?*

➤ *How many houses/condos/co-ops/town houses have you sold in the past year?*

➤ *Which neighborhoods are you most familiar with?*

➤ *Do you have any recommendation letters from clients?*

➤ *What are you looking for in a client?*

The answer to that last question can be quite telling. Most never hear it, and their answer will suggest whether they have thought about it very much. Professional real estate salespeople know exactly what qualities they want in a client and can articulate them. If the answers fit your requirements, you may have the right salesperson.

Some books tell you that the place to meet a real estate agent is at an open house. That may not be the best advice, for many reasons. The agent is there to represent the seller first. Depending on how busy the open house is, you may be competing for the agent's time, with interruptions as other guests come in, ask questions, and pick up objects they aren't supposed to. The agent can't focus on helping you with your housing needs if distracted. Still, an open house does make a good place to watch a candidate agent at work. How does the agent handle visitors? What does the agent do when not busy? What questions does the agent ask you? If you are interested further, make an appointment to talk alone with the agent.

Insider's Tip

Most professional agents specialize in working with properties in one or a group of neighborhoods they call a "farm." They keep up on all new listings, pending sales, and potential listings in that area. For obvious reasons, you want to work with an agent who farms in the neighborhoods you're most interested in. You can often find them by driving the neighborhoods and keeping track of who has the most FOR SALE signs. Remember, however, that these agents may be more skilled at working with sellers than buyers.

Once you've narrowed down the field to one or two agents you think will best help you, call them to make an appointment for a showing. What's a showing? It's an opportunity for an agent to show you how they help buyers. A typical showing will include a short qualifying interview in which the agent determines your needs and price range, followed by the selecting and showing of a few properties that fit your stated requirements. In many cases, the agent will qualify you over the phone, then set an appointment for sometime within the next seventy-two hours for a tour of selected homes. If you identify a specific neighborhood with which the agent is familiar, you may get taken on the tour right then.

Unless there are few homes for sale in your marketplace and price range, chances are you're not going to buy one of the first properties you see. The showing is more an opportunity for you to find out more about the agent—and for the agent to find out more about you! You're asking yourself: *Is this an agent whom I trust to find and help me buy the home that best fits my requirements?* Meantime, the agent is asking: *Are these buyers who won't waste my time and efforts on their behalf?* You're each going to spend time, energy, and money on each other. Think of the first showing as the first date.

Insider's Tip

If you have seen a specific property with another agent, say so as soon as you realize it. A good agent will want to know this. She probably will ask you if you are also having that agent show you property, and if you want to use his services to purchase your home. If the answer is yes, then she will say good-bye. If your answer is no, then the agent will continue working with you as your exclusive agent. She will ask you if you would like her to phone the other agent to tell him, or if you will tell the other agent (if he's still calling you).

As a first "date," a showing is subject to all the problems that can occur early in a relationship: anticipation, miscommunication, misreading, and bad starts. Often, however, it's an indicator of what will follow. An agent who sensitively asks good questions and finds properties that fit stated requirements should be hired. Fortunately, you read chapter 4 and know many of the things you want in your next home and you've communicated them to the agent.

Hiring the Best

How does a buyer hire an agent, who typically works for the seller? Unless the salesperson is a buyer's agent or dual agent, there's no hiring agreement you sign. It's a verbal agreement based on the agent's question: *If I bring you a property that fits your stated requirements, will you attempt to purchase it through me?* If your answer is yes, you have a verbal agreement to hire. Alternatively, you can make a similar statement to the agent: *If you bring me a property that fits my stated requirements, I will attempt to purchase it through you.*

Insider's Tip

What are good agents supposed to do for you? They use their knowledge and skills to present you with the best real estate options and help you come to a decision that matches your actual requirements.

Unfortunately, many agents and many buyers *assume* the answer to this question. Though verbal agreements regarding real estate are *not legally binding,* they do form an understanding between the agent and the buyer. Believe me, agents will work harder for a buyer with whom they have such an agreement or understanding. They know that their efforts will probably be rewarded by a commission, so they are more willing to work harder for you, the buyer.

Summary

To get one of the best real estate agents you can find, take a little time to do your homework toward identifying the better brokers and salespeople, interviewing them to make sure they will work hard for you. Are they willing to go the extra mile for you? Then clarify your relationship so the selected agent knows that professional efforts will be rewarded. Any other method of finding an agent is hit-and-miss. You're spending too much money and time to entrust your home search to a dud.

CHAPTER 7

Helping Your Agent Work Harder

*C*ongratulations! You've selected the *right* agent to help you buy your next home. You've found an agent who is willing to trade knowledgeable service for the probability of a commission check. If you are serious about this transaction and willing to work cooperatively with your agent, you will find that buying a home is relatively easy. It's all about service!

Knowing Your Agent

Being a *good* agent isn't the easiest job in the world. In fact, it's quite difficult—*if* the agent attempts to give good and knowledgeable service to clients. A professional agent's workweek typically is long, often reducing family and recreation time. There's no one to tell the agent when to start work or when to stop. Phone calls come at all hours of all days. Deals may fall apart because other agents in the transaction don't work professionally. Or agents lose commissions because a buyer or seller isn't honest or accurate about important facts.

Unfortunately, some take shortcuts that jeopardize the assets of others. Shortcuts are okay as long as they don't change the outcome. It's called working efficiently. And that's one key to being a good agent: efficiency. Even mediocre agents can become professionals if they learn how to work efficiently. Efficient agents know how to use time productively, how to learn about the greatest number of properties in the shortest time, how to identify qualified buyers, how to show homes, and how to help buyers find lenders who also work efficiently and professionally. An

> ## Insider's Tip
>
> Being honest with your agent means being accurate with yourself. Do you need four bedrooms in your next home? If so, consider why and what you would do if you found the perfect home except it had three bedrooms. If you'd opt for fewer bedrooms, how important is four bedrooms compared to other factors? Chapter 4 offered guidelines on getting the home you want, but as you begin looking at properties your priorities may change. That's okay; you're becoming more accurate in defining your housing needs.

efficient agent can make twice or three times as much money as an inefficient one who otherwise has the same skills and knowledge. An efficient agent will also reduce stress on you and transaction time. The agent you selected probably knows this; you probably recognized it in him or her. The key to success in real estate is efficiency, also known as time management.

So the first chance you get in your relationship, you should learn more about your selected agent. You know the basics, but you may not know much about the agent as a person. Why is this important? Because credentials don't sell homes—people do. Once you understand your agent better, you can help her or him do the job better. You can bring your skills and preferences to the relationship and find the right home faster and easier. That's your ultimate goal.

Letting Your Agent Know You

Conversely, your agent needs to know more about you to help identify the best home for your needs. A good agent may ask or you can volunteer facts about your lifestyle that will be reflected in your home:

➤ Your home history (houses, apartments, styles, locations).

➤ Your home preference (larger, smaller, comfortable, prestige, close to work).

➤ Number of children, genders, and ages.

➤ Pet types and where they live (indoors, outdoors, garage).

➤ Number and type of vehicles (commuter cars, classic cars, recreation vehicles, boats, ATVs, and so on).

➤ Special interests, hobbies, pastimes, and how your home should accommodate them.

➤ How you prefer to make major decisions (alone, with partners, with parents or other relatives, whomever).

Insider's Tip

What motivates a good agent? Commissions are probably number one; we all must make a living. Better agents, however, are also motivated by the need to be of service to others. They know that good service equates with commissions, so they take care of the service and their clients will take care of them. To better know agents, ask what motivates them—then watch to see if it's true.

The next part of knowing your needs is prioritizing them. Help your agent understand what is *most* important in your decision to buy. It may be to move to a better neighborhood, to be closer to work, to remove equity from an existing property and downsize to a condo, or to find a retirement home now that the kids have moved away. Of course, make sure that you and other decision makers in your living group agree to the prioritization. For example, school district may come first, then garage size.

Working with Your Agent

Your agent has already told you how she or he prefers to work with buyers (chapter 6), and you've agreed on the general terms. Now it's time to work out any bugs so that your time and your agent's time are most efficiently used. Your agent may offer to contact any FSBOs you see on your behalf. You may offer to

Pitfall

Some advisers tell you not to show all your cards to the agent. *Don't let the agent know how much you can spend on a house,* they say. That's bad advice. If you don't tell the agent this important fact, how can the agent determine what to show you? Let your agent go with you to the lender to determine exactly how much you can afford. That way you will not waste time looking at homes out of your price range, falling in love with a home you cannot afford, and then not being satisfied with the home you can afford. Playing games is okay with Monopoly money, but not with *your* money. Instead, let the agent you trust know—and help you verify—your price range (chapter 8).

Insider's Tip

Here's something that people outside the real estate industry probably don't know. The homes-for-sale ads in the paper really aren't intended to sell you the advertised home! In fact, they have multiple functions—from showing the seller that the agent is marketing the property to acting as bait to attract new buyers in the market. There's too little information in the ad (intentionally!) to tell buyers if it is worth considering, so the buyer calls the listing agent and, bingo, the agent has a new client. Instead, most agents prefer to work the new listings on the market—the ones that won't be in the paper for a few weeks—seeking homes to show you. Let them. Once your agent understands what you are looking for, ask the agent to "preview" properties that meet your criteria. This will save you both time.

scan the daily or weekly real estate ads and request more information on specific advertised properties. Or your agent may agree to give you "drive-by" addresses for you to view from the road before deciding whether you want to take a look inside.

How the agent works with you depends somewhat on how much time you have. If you must be in a new home in thirty days, the agent may meet with you every day for a few hours going over the options and visiting properties. If you have more time, the agent may set up a weekly or twice-a-week appointment to show you the latest homes that match your requirements. The more serious you seem about buying, the more seriously most agents will invest their time and money to help you.

Insider's Tip

Want your agent to be loyal to you, bringing you the best deals as soon as they hit the market? Then be loyal to her or him, working exclusively through that agent. Don't call all around town to various real estate offices asking questions. See something you want more information about? Ask your exclusive agent.

When and How to Ask

As you work with your agent, numerous questions will arise regarding neighborhoods, financing, the buying process, a specific property, and other topics. When should you ask them? It's typically best to save your questions for a face-to-face meeting if possible. If not, try not to deluge your agent with telephone calls asking one question at a time. Save them up. And the best way of doing so is keeping a Buyer's Notebook, a steno or other small notebook for recording questions, telephone numbers, properties toured, and other facts. Keep the questions in a separate part of the book and check them off as they are answered. Some of them you will answer as you learn more about buying a home. Others should be asked of your agent—and you should make sure you understand the answer.

Good answers come from good questions. Think your questions through and write them down as clearly as possible. Instead of "What about the Jones condo?" ask, "We looked at the Jones condo on March 11 and I still have a question: Is the master bedroom sufficiently large to hold our bedroom set?" Such a question will get you a specific and useful answer. In addition, it will be easier to ask because you may not remember what you were thinking when you wrote, "What about the Jones condo?"

Insider's Tip

Good agents *love* good questions. Not only does it make their job of answering them easier, it also gives the agents an opportunity to ask a qualifying question, as appropriate. "If the Joneses' master bedroom is sufficiently large for your bedroom set, are you ready to make an offer?" Know that agents often do this and be ready with an answer so you're not caught off guard.

What's a good question? It's one that identifies its context and requires a specific answer: "Yes," "No," "180 square feet," "The deck will hold up to forty people." Why is context important? Not only does it help refresh your memory as to the source of the question, but it helps the agent give a more accurate answer—because the agent probably has seen dozens of properties with various buyers since then and may need a reminder.

When and How to Tell

You're going to be looking at properties together, you and your agent. How can you help your agent better understand what you're looking for? Offer clear feedback. Feedback is an informative response.

For example, once you both leave a home or apartment you've toured together, make a point of telling the agent your primary and secondary impressions in a way that will help him or her understand what you're looking for. You could say the living room is adequate but the bedrooms are too small. Or the house is fine but the neighborhood is not what you prefer. Be as specific as possible. I'll give you some more guidelines in chapter 9 on interviewing properties.

Remember to keep track of showings, feedback, questions, and responses in your Buyer's Notebook.

Relieving Buyer's Anxiety

Homes are expensive. They typically cost many years of income. Add in mortgage interest and you can see where about one-third of your income will go for the next fifteen to thirty years.

Homes also change lives. Buying a home in one neighborhood over another can determine the schools kids go to, the jobs you accept, the new friends you find, and your day-to-day living. Scary, huh?

On the other side of the coin is the investment you are making. Even in slow economies, homes are one of the best investments you can make. They appreciate in total value—not just your down payment. You are leveraging your initial investment and earning more on it than you can through nearly any other simple (buy it, sit back, sell it) investments. And how many other investments do you get to live in?

So why do people feel that this is such a difficult decision? Because there are too many options! Buy here. Buy there. Mortgage rates are moving. The local economy is fluctuating. A prison may be built nearby. There are just so many details that must be considered before buying one specific house or apartment. It's buyer's anxiety.

That's where a good professional real estate salesperson can really help. An experienced agent has been through many home sales and purchases, has seen numerous changes in the local economy and the national mortgage rates, and knows that, if done properly, buying a home doesn't have to be stressful. It's a well-defined process with many traps that can be avoided with knowledge and a little hard work. Knowing how to help that agent do the best job for you is *your* job.

Summary

Hiring a real estate agent requires developing a business relationship. It's based on identified needs, communication skills, mutual trust, and, of course, a professional attitude of service. You can help your agent work harder for you by helping him or her understand your housing requirements through clear communication. Some extra effort on your part can find you a better home faster and maybe at a lower cost.

CHAPTER 8

Getting the Money First

*O*ne of the most frustrating situations in buying real estate is falling in love with a home that fits your needs, but doesn't fit your wallet. Unfortunately, many buyers get caught in this trap, because of either not knowing the marketplace or getting bad advice. They may give up and rent, or take on financing that they really can't afford.

The solution is to get your money first! It's like making sure you have enough in your wallet *before* walking into an expensive restaurant. Even if you're paying cash for the home, you want to make sure you have *enough* cash. Buying with financing is like buying with cash except that the lender writes the check, not you. So it makes sense to first find out how much of a check the lender will write—and make sure you can afford to make the payments.

Getting Smarter About Real Estate Finance

Chapter 3 covered the basics of residential home finance: how the money market works, how lenders work, the basics of mortgages. On that foundation, this chapter shows you how to get prequalified for a home mortgage so you know what you can comfortably buy.

The first step in educating yourself about real estate finance is reviewing what you already know. If you currently have a mortgage, dig out the paperwork—that thick envelope of papers you got when the sale closed. One of the more important documents in that package is the Truth in Lending Disclosure Statement

(TILDS). If you don't have a prior mortgage, here's what it's about. The TILDS includes:

➤ Annual percentage rate.

➤ Amount financed.

➤ Finance charge.

➤ Total amount of payments.

➤ Number of payments.

➤ When payments start and stop.

➤ Other loan info: late charges, prepayment option, mortgage insurance, prepayment penalty, assumability, loan number, and so forth.

Most important to you in the short term are the annual percentage rate (APR) and the payment amount. You obviously want the lowest APR you can get, and you need to know when to pay to avoid late charges.

Lingo

Annual percentage rate (APR) is the effective (actual) rate of interest for a loan, per year. It includes *all* interest charges for the loan as well as *points* or prepaid interest. It is the cost of your credit as a yearly rate. Use the APR to compare actual interest rates among various lenders.

The TILDS includes the total amount you will pay if you make all payments as scheduled. It's the monthly payment amount times the number of payments. To determine how much of it is interest, deduct the amount financed. For example, if you have a fifteen-year mortgage at $1,200 a month, the total is $216,000 (180 × $1,200). If you're financing $150,000 (the principal), the difference of $66,000 is the total interest. The $216,000 is the principal *and* interest (PI).

Your Financial Options

You have many options when financing a residence. You don't have to use a mortgage lender. In fact, many thousands of properties are purchased every year without a traditional mortgage lender. What other options are available?

➤ Assume payments on the property's existing mortgage (subject to its conditions).

➤ Make mortgage payments directly to the seller as an installment sale.

➤ Make first mortgage payments to the lender and second mortgage payments to the seller.

➤ Exchange the equity in your home for a comparable equity in another home with an agreeable seller.

Why would you consider purchasing a home with a nontraditional mortgage lender? Maybe your credit rating isn't sufficient to get the mortgage you want. Maybe the seller would prefer to get payments rather than a lump sum and can offer an attractive interest rate. Maybe you can get a mortgage, but not one big enough to buy, so the seller offers to take a *second mortgage* for the balance.

The point here is that you aren't limited to conventional financing when buying your house or apartment. In most cases, however, there will be a mortgage involved (unless you pay cash). Remember that a mortgage is a legal document that creates a lien (or right) against real estate as security toward payment of a specified debt. Lending institutions can hold a mortgage, but so can the seller or your Uncle Harry. In fact, the seller or Uncle Harry may not be as stringent when it comes to your credit, and may not charge you loan fees!

nspectors A
scrow Pr
ntinge
Title
ell

Lingo

A *second mortgage* is a lien against the property that is second or subordinate to the rights of the first mortgage lien.

Prequalifying

To qualify for a loan means to get approval based on your credit history, earning power, and other assets, specifically your debt-to-income ratio. To *prequalify* simply means to get approval before you have a specific property in mind. Prequalifying makes good sense because you then know what you can get rather than guessing. In fact, you can use prequalifying as an opportunity to not only get preapproval, but also do some horse trading. If you're prequalified through one lender at a set loan amount and a specific interest rate, you can typically get another lender to make you a better offer. Besides, you're going to go through the qualifying process anyway, so why not get it out of the way early?

Chapter 3 mentioned the URLA or Uniform Residential Loan Application, a standardized loan app that most mortgage brokers, bankers, and other housing lenders require. Even your Uncle Harry may require it before lending you money. The URLA includes:

➤ The type of mortgage.

➤ The terms of the loan.

➤ Property information (leave this blank for now) and purpose of the loan.

➤ Information about the borrower and any co-borrower (spouse, whoever).

➤ Employment information about the borrower and co-borrower.

➤ Monthly income and combined housing expense information.

➤ A list and valuation of all assets (what you own, including variables such as life insurance, stocks, 401(k), and IRA) and liabilities (what you owe, including credit cards and student loans).

➤ The details of the transaction (if known).

➤ Lots of fine print.

Insider's Tip

Some lenders won't accept a loan application until you have a specific property in mind. Most, however, will let you fill out an unofficial loan app and, based on this, tell you what loan you will probably qualify for. There's no commitment made, but you have an indicator of what you can probably do. Think of it as a dress rehearsal for your full loan app.

The URLA is standardized to make it easy for a loan officer to make a quick decision based on the facts it includes.

What is the lender looking for? Each lender will have different guidelines, depending on how conservative or aggressive its lending rules are, your credit score, and other factors. Many, however, use the 28–36 qualifying ratio. That is, the total monthly payment (principal, interest, taxes, and insurance, or PITI) must be 28 percent or less of the total income, *and* the total of all your debts must be 36 percent or less of total income. This obviously means that if you don't have any car payments or other big debts, you can go to the higher number. In addition, if you have a high asset ratio (lots more assets than liabilities) you may be able to get an even larger mortgage. Remember, your down payment will come into this evaluation. If you can put more money down, you will have smaller monthly payments, your interest rate will be lower, and you may not need mortgage insurance.

Insider's Tip

It's better for you if the loan officer fills out the application for you, because she or he can help you avoid misinterpretation and undervaluation. Most folks actually undervalue their personal assets, especially household goods. You may find that loan officers estimate your household assets at twice what you may. That's because they are looking at full replacement value.

Pitfall

Beware of the too-large mortgage. Just because a lender will loan you a specified amount doesn't mean you can comfortably pay it back. You may know more about the industry in which you work and how the job market may change in the coming years, or may want to keep the mortgage lower so you can finance college educations soon. It's you, *not* the lender, who will be writing the monthly check, so make sure it's a check you *can* write.

To give you an example, someone with a $60,000 annual gross income should be able to qualify for a mortgage (PITI) of $1,800 a month (36 percent of $5,000 a month) *less* any other long-term (more than one year) debts. So the lower the interest rate, the higher the mortgage amount can be. Also, lower property taxes mean you can qualify for a larger mortgage. Add to this the down payment and you know about how much home you can afford.

The lender also is looking at the loan-to-value (LTV) ratio, the amount borrowed compared to the property value. If you get a mortgage loan of $160,000 to buy a $200,000 home, the LTV ratio is 80 percent. If the LTV is greater than 80 percent, the lender will probably require that you buy mortgage insurance, an additional expense. The difference between the loan amount and the property value is your *equity* in the house or apartment.

Checking Your Credit

Maybe you have great credit. Maybe not. Or if you're like most people, you're not sure. Did that late credit card payment last year show up? Has an error crept into your credit report, making it difficult to finance a house or apartment? Find out now, *before* you go shopping!

To know what your credit is like, you'll first need a *real* credit report issued by a *real* credit reporting agency. Here are some of the major players:

➤ Equifax, www.equifax.com, 800-685-1111.

➤ Experian (previously TRW), www.experian.com, 888-397-3742.

➤ TransUnion, www.transunion.com, 800-888-4213.

You can buy a copy of your credit report from each of these three major players—or any one of them will sell you a combined credit report from its database and from the other two. One-stop shopping. In addition, you can get your "credit score" and an explanation of what it means. Most lenders will take the average of all three credit reporting agencies, not just the highest one.

Why do you want a copy of your credit report *now*? Because whatever lender you use will certainly order one (at your expense) when your loan app is submitted. It just makes good sense to see what they will see *before* they do. There may be a forgotten credit card problem or an erroneous credit claim, or someone else's report mixed in with yours.

Pitfall

How about a *free credit report*? Nothing is really free. Some of the services that offer free credit reports really want you to take a loan through them, and they will let you see a copy of your credit report for free. Of course, loan fees will include the cost of the credit report—but you get a free peek! Other pitfalls are built around "free" credit reports. Pay for it yourself (typically about $10 to $20 each, or less in combination) and don't get scammed. Remember that every time you request a credit report, it actually lowers your credit score.

Credit reports today include a credit score, often the one developed by Fair Isaac Corporation called the FICO score. Why should you care about your credit score? Because lenders do! They look at many factors, but your credit score is perceived as an accurate snapshot of your credit rating. In plain English: The higher your credit score, the lower the interest rate you may be offered. So it's really to your advantage to not only know your credit score, but also do everything you legally can do to raise it!

What's your credit score based on? The FICO system calculates relative scores based on your payment history, how much credit you have, how long you've had that credit, how much new credit you've gotten recently, and what mix of credit you have (long-term, short-term, and so on). You can learn more about FICO scores by requesting *Understanding Your Credit Score* from Fair Isaac Corporation (www.myfico.com).

What can you do to improve your overall credit rating and your credit score?

Insider's Tip

To get a mortgage through most lenders, you will need a FICO score of at least 680. That makes you a prime borrower. Less than 680 means you are considered subprime and will have to pay more interest, but chances are that you can still get a mortgage. If your score is below 550, you'll need some credit repair before any reputable lender (even a credit card company) will loan you money.

➤ Get a copy of your credit history and credit score.

➤ Verify that the information is correct (including addresses), contacting the appropriate credit reporting bureau to make needed corrections.

➤ Don't open any new credit card or store accounts (you get a higher score for active accounts that are at least eighteen months old).

➤ Close any old accounts that you no longer use; if you have few credit accounts, consider reactivating older accounts with a small purchase.

➤ If there are any "charge-offs" or unpaid bad debts, contact the lender (not the credit reporting bureau) to find out how to get them removed from your report.

➤ Wait for a month if possible until all of the changes and corrections are reported to the credit bureaus, then order a new copy of your current credit history and credit score. Remember that every time someone orders a credit check, your FICO score goes down slightly.

➤ Once you've applied for a mortgage, if possible don't get any new credit cards or other loans until the sale is closed and recorded.

Summary

The smartest thing you can do when buying a house or apartment is find out first what you can afford to buy. That means knowing about Truth in Lending, your financial options, prequalifying, and cleaning up your credit *before* going shopping. Then you can confidently match your housing needs and your income to make a purchase you can really live with.

CHAPTER 9

Interviewing Property

*F*or most of us with limited funds, the perfect home isn't for sale. If you have a budget of millions, you might be able to find that perfect home with all the amenities you ever wanted or ever will want. The rest of us compromise.

Compromise is okay. Chances are we really don't need two Olympic swimming pools anyway. Instead, we select the amenities that we most want and look for them within our budget. If you have a smart real estate agent, she or he will help you determine your needs and what you can compromise on, then show it to you. Mediocre agents will waste your time and theirs by showing you homes that don't fit your needs and budget.

That's what this chapter is all about: interviewing properties to determine if they fit your needs and budget. A good agent makes the job much easier.

Getting the Facts

Buying a house can be an emotional decision, but it should be based primarily on facts: what you need, what's available, and what you have to trade for it. Chapter 4 guided you through the definition process to help you determine the size, type, location, and price range of the home you're looking for. This chapter is about getting the facts and inspecting candidate properties. To keep your facts straight, I suggest you gather a few tools.

First, make sure you have your Buyer's Notebook with you as you interview properties. It can be a spiral notebook, a PDA, or any other tool for gathering information. As suggested in chapter 4, it gives you a handy repository for facts: housing needs, names and numbers, specific property details, observations, and other useful info.

One of the facts that many buyers forget to ask about is property taxes and special assessments. Depending on where you're buying, these can be insignificant (meaning schools and services may not be adequately funded) or excessive (meaning you're paying too much for what you are getting). Of course, you can't move the home you purchase to a different tax district, but you really need to know how much taxes are—and will be—as you consider specific properties. Remember: Every dollar paid for property taxes reduces the mortgage you can get by a dollar (see chapter 8).

As you drive around various neighborhoods and properties, you may get disoriented—or just plain lost. If you have a good sense of direction, you may be able to stay oriented. If not, consider buying a small compass or referring to one in your car if it is so equipped. Location of the sun, major thoroughfares, work, and school relative to your next home can be important.

A measuring tape or two also is a good investment for inspecting properties. I recommend a twenty-five-foot tape for interior measurements and a hundred-foot tape for measuring property lines (unless they are obvious). If you want to make the job easier, consider a laser tape, a digital device that can quickly measure room walls and even tell you how many square feet are in the room. They are relatively inexpensive. Alternatively, your real estate agent may have one.

Another gadget for your inspections is a quality flashlight. With it, you can easily view attics, unlit basements and crawl spaces, garage storage, what's under decks, and anywhere else that there isn't sufficient light to see what you may be getting. A flashlight also is handy for inspecting a ceiling for water marks that may not otherwise show up.

One last tip before getting on with the actual inspections: Visit a home improvement center. What are you looking for? Prices!

Insider's Tip

Before going out and buying a compass, tape measure, and flashlight, ask your agent if he or she has them. If so, ask the agent to make sure they are available when you inspect properties.

Take a look at the cost of a new sink, carpeting, bathroom cabinets, paint, and other replacement products, writing them in your Buyer's Notebook. Why? As you go through a property and see a damaged sink, flooring, or cabinet, you'll have an idea of what it will cost to replace it. If you'd rather not do the actual replacement yourself, double the cost as the installed price. It's an approximation, of course, but it will tell you whether a few gallons of paint and some replacement materials will turn an almost-right home into the right one.

Sizing Up Drive-Bys

As you begin looking at specific properties, you may see homes for sale in your selected neighborhoods or be directed to a specific address by your agent. Many agents offer drive-by addresses if they are comfortable with your allegiance to them and if you seem comfortable with doing some of the legwork.

Insider's Tip

If your agent has given you a fresh drive-by that has been listed in the last forty-eight hours, ask the agent to be available for an immediate showing if you like the property. If the drive-by tells you that you want to see more, call the agent and get a walk-through before other buyers and agents see it.

There are many things you can tell about the interior of a home in just a drive-by. The first thing to look for is window placement and size. Tall windows typically indicate the location of a living room or great room. Short windows above the middle of a wall often indicate a bedroom. If the window is smaller and higher on the wall, it is probably a bathroom. Small windows below the main floor of the house suggest a basement.

Also take a look at the roof. A dormer with window indicates a second-story room, usually a bedroom. A chimney marks the location of a fireplace. A vent pipe often signifies that a bathroom or kitchen is below.

Of course, also visually inspect the front or curb view of the house or apartment, but don't be misled. Listing agents stress that sellers should dress up the front of their home with plants, extra maintenance, and ornaments to help develop *curb appeal*, a term referring to how the home looks from the curb. You may find that the side of the home or the rear has not been attended to and more accurately reflects the home's condition.

Pitfall

What you see may not be what you get. Some sellers will adorn the front of their home with ornamental potted plants and other decorations that are not attached to the house or the land. As you learned in chapter 1, these elements are personal, not real, property, and are not part of the sale unless specifically included in the agreement.

Walking Through

Walking through and inspecting houses and apartments for sale can be fun—if you don't feel you are encroaching on the seller's privacy. You're not! In fact, the sellers want lots of buyers looking at their home *if* the buyers remember that they are guests. Look but don't touch. Your real estate agent (hired by the seller, remember) watches to make sure buyers don't touch what they shouldn't. In most cases, they allow you to open room doors, cabinet doors, and other entries, but not to remove personal items. If you need to see the plumbing under the sink, ask the agent to stand nearby as you do so. Or ask the seller or the agent to take a look for you.

Insider's Tip

How many properties should you walk through during a single tour? It depends on how well your agent knows what you are looking for and how much time you have. To educate yourself and your agent, you may look at half a dozen properties in an afternoon, giving feedback to the agent on each. The agent may then set up longer showings for just two or three properties selected because they closely match the definition of what you're looking for.

Insider's Tip

If you're not careful, the homes you look at will begin to run together in your mind. Did the one on Pinecone Drive have a single or double garage? Which one had the bathroom that needed new tile? For this reason, I strongly recommend that you take your Buyer's Notebook with you whenever you tour properties. Also ask for and staple the listing sheet to your notes about that property. And refer to your notebook to remind you what to look for in each property.

In some cases, the current residents (seller or renter) will be in the house, though most agents discourage them from doing so. If introduced, greet them, then pretty much ignore them until you have specific questions to ask. Don't try to impress them, or let them try to impress you. Just go about your inspection of the house. Remember to share your comments with the agent and your other decision makers *after* you have left the residence so you can't be overheard. Also remember that "your" agent probably works for the seller.

Most property tours or walk-throughs start at the main entrance and move toward the back door. Use your Buyer's Notebook to make a rough sketch of the home's layout. If you're not good at drawing, make a circle for each room relative to other rooms and label it. You'll probably refer to the drawing many times later if the house becomes a contender.

The seller can be a wealth of information—or misinformation. If the seller is at the home during the tour, ask the agent a question that only the seller can answer. At this point, the agent may draw the seller into the conversation and you can ask further questions regarding neighborhood, recent repairs, needed repairs, and (very important) motivation for selling. You also may get the seller to tell you how long the property has been on the market. If the seller is not at home, you can ask the agent for a conference call with the seller to respond to questions the agent can't answer. Of course, some agents may be protective of the seller, telling you they'll ask the seller and get back to you.

Insider's Tip

Want to impress a seller and gain a possible advantage in negotiations? Show an interest in the seller's hobbies, children, or pets. By making a positive impression, you become more memorable than the faces-without-names that have toured the property. A conversation on a common interest not only gives you a chance to learn more about the property, but also makes you a person whom the seller prefers as a buyer. It won't hurt. And believe me, if sellers don't *like* you, some won't sell to you at full price.

Reinspecting Choices

Once you've narrowed the field down to two to four best properties, it's time to reinspect them before making an offer on the best one. Reinspection means taking a second look at things you may not have been clear on as well as taking a first look at things you forgot to check the first time. The initial tour may have been for thirty to sixty minutes; a reinspection can take two or more hours, depending on the home's size and condition. (Obviously, a brand-new home won't take as long to inspect as an older remodeled home.) If allowed, take a film, digital, or video camera with you to capture the residence for future referral.

If you have questions you can't answer about the plumbing, electrical, framing, or other systems, you may want to hire a professional housing inspector. However, don't do so yet. If you have concerns, check as much as you can without an inspector. Why? Because you are going to make your offer to purchase subject to the results of a professional inspection, a pest and fungus inspection, septic inspection, roof inspection, title inspection, and any other reasonable inspection you can muster up. You'll learn why in the next chapter.

Insider's Tip

When can you see the seller's disclosure statement (chapter 2)? In most states, it must be provided to you at the time you make an offer or within a specified period after that offer, such as seventy-two hours. Once you've seen it, you can accept it—or reject it and stop the deal, called the *right of recision*. Still, you can also see the disclosure statement *before* you make an offer if you wish, though you will then lose your right of recision. In fact, you can ask your agent to provide a copy of the disclosure statement for any home you look at. Remember, it's the seller's opinion of the facts, not necessarily the facts.

In many states, the buying process will include a buyer's inspection advisory, a form that you must read and sign when making your offer. It gives you clues as to what should be inspected:

➤ General condition of the property and structure.

➤ Soil stability.

➤ Structure size and age.

➤ Pest control.

➤ Roof condition.

➤ Water system (utility service or well).

➤ Waste disposal (sewer or septic).

➤ Environmental hazards (asbestos, lead paint, radon, and so on).

➤ Earthquake and flood hazards.

➤ Building permits.

➤ Safety and security.

➤ Neighborhood nuisances.

➤ Zoning laws and requirements.

➤ Title issues (road maintenance agreements, easements, et cetera).

When you hire a professional inspection service later, it will check all of these elements for you and issue a report. Most focus on structural systems (heating, plumbing, electrical, waste, roof, water, septic) and pest control, identifying damage and the presence of infestations. If any of these components has serious problems, a specialized contractor may be called in to assess damage and offer a cost bid to repair it. By making a final and professional inspection a part of your offer, you will give yourself an opportunity to discontinue the sale if the inspection turns up more problems than you or the sellers are willing to resolve.

What should you be looking for in your reinspection? Anything you may have missed or weren't sure of in your first inspection. Check for:

➤ Damp or smelly basement.

➤ Discolored spots on the walls or ceilings.

➤ Water spots around windows, skylights, and doors.

➤ Amateur electrical work, bare wires, or obvious burns on electrical receptacles.

➤ Foggy windows, especially double-pane windows.

➤ Bad smells in the home, especially a home with carpeting and pets.

➤ Damp attic.

➤ Obvious insect damage to the exterior, such as sawdust trails or large nests.

➤ Furnace and ducting condition.

➤ Ceiling repairs (which may indicate a roof or second-story leak).

Make notes on any of these problems in your Buyer's Notebook and make sure you discuss them with the agent and, if necessary, the home inspector. If at all possible, be at the house when the home inspector makes the inspection. If you can't attend, ask your agent to be there. That bad smell may be from cooking foods you're not accustomed to, or it may be caused by moisture and mold. Write it down and ask.

Summary

A mortgage is a fact, not an opinion. The purchase of a specific home should be based primarily on facts, not opinions. You can gather the needed facts by interviewing properties, keeping good notes, and finding out whatever you can about a specific property before making an offer to buy. You can then make a smart decision that will fulfill your housing and financial needs.

CHAPTER 10

Making the Offer

*C*ongratulations! You've found a home you can live with. With the help of your real estate agent, you've developed the criteria, reviewed the options, and selected one or two properties that best fit your needs and budget. Now it's time to make an offer to the seller.

This is the part of the transaction where a good agent shines—and a mediocre one falls apart. Fortunately, you've done your homework toward selecting the best agent to help you. Even so, remember that, in most real estate transactions, the agent actually works for the *seller*. It's to the agent's advantage to get you to offer the highest price you can. More commission! By knowing how the offer is made and what control you have over it, you can protect your interests while getting the home you want.

Offer to Purchase

Your offer to purchase a specific property is made by the real estate agent on your behalf. You can have a lawyer draw it up instead or use standardized forms from a stationery store, but most agents use the forms published by the state or local real estate association.

The forms have various titles, such as Residential Purchase Agreement, Earnest Money Agreement, and Real Estate Purchase Agreement. Some forms cover all types of real estate transactions (houses and apartments, vacant land, commercial), while others cover one type. In this book, I'll call the form the Residential Purchase Agreement or RPA.

What does the RPA cover?

➤ The offer (property description and purchase price).

➤ How it will be paid (cash, financing).

➤ When the sale will close and when the new owners can occupy the property.

➤ Allocation of costs (who pays for what inspections and closing costs).

➤ Hazard disclosures (lead paint, asbestos, natural hazards).

➤ Condition of the property (as is, subject to seller repairs, with homeowner warranty).

➤ What personal property is included and excluded from the sale.

➤ Information on any property the buyer must sell before finalizing the purchase of the subject residence.

➤ Additional contingencies and their time limits.

➤ How any disputes will be resolved.

➤ Some legal stuff about the seller offering clear title to the property.

➤ Some legal definitions.

➤ Instructions to the escrow agent on how to produce closing documents.

➤ Places for everyone to initial each page and sign the document.

➤ Additional disclosures for property lines, septic systems, wells, and so forth.

In some states, the RPA is just a couple of legal pages long, with addendums for special terms and conditions. Many states include the addendums within the document, making it up to ten pages long! Multiply this by at least three copies (buyer, seller, escrow), and you can see that making an offer isn't as simple as writing a price down on a piece of paper. RPAs have evolved over the years to become extensive documents designed to protect all the parties from lawsuits—especially the agents.

Tips Tips
Tips
Tips T:
Tips
ps

Insider's Tip

You don't have to wait until you're ready to make an offer to see an RPA form. Ask your agent to provide one to you or pick up a standardized one at a stationery store early in the process and study it as you can. Make notes and ask questions. The more you know about the home-buying process, the better you'll come out.

Including Contingencies

A contingency is a condition. It would be simple if everyone purchased homes with all cash, the homes were in perfect condition, and date of occupancy could be worked out verbally. Of course, life isn't that simple. Financing is required. The house or apartment should be inspected for pests, damage, and health hazards before buying. Moving vans need some notice before showing up. That's why RPAs include contingency clauses. The sale can go through *if* other things first occur: The buyer qualifies for a mortgage, inspections are passed, the home appraises at a specific value.

Contingencies are often written to protect the buyer. If you can't get the loan, if the house doesn't pass inspection, or you can't move in by a specified date, you may not want the house. So write any requirements you have in your Buyer's Notebook and discuss them with your agent. They may become conditions to the sale.

Some RPAs have a paragraph to cover any possible contingency, while others use addendums for contingencies that must be written in by the agents. For example, you can include a condition that you'll only buy the house if you can get a Veterans

Administration (VA) loan on it, or if you can get a conventional loan at under a specific interest rate. You can rescind the offer if an appraisal isn't at least the purchase price. Or you can cancel your offer if the pest inspection shows damage requiring repairs above a specific amount. You don't *have* to cancel your offer, but you can. A smart agent will make sure you have contingencies in the RPA, but not ones so broad that you can cancel on a whim. Remember that contingencies will have deadlines, and make sure you and your agent know what they are.

Insider's Tip

About the time it looks like there will be an agreement between buyer and seller, agents will ask you to sign something called an Agency Disclosure. It outlines what a seller's agent, a buyer's agent, and an agent representing both seller and buyer are required to do. *It does not tell you which type of agent you have!* It's up to you to ask and to understand. This is often the first form you sign—even before making your offer.

Making the Offer to Buy

The first question many buyers ask is: *How much below the asking price can I offer?* Of course, your agent probably wants you to make a full-price offer that will quickly get accepted and earn a commission. You may or may not get much help from your agent on the offer amount, so here are some guidelines. The agent cannot legally tell you a lower amount to offer, but can make general statements such as, *The sellers have said they are very firm on the price but may be negotiable on appliances,* or, *The sellers are in escrow on another house and are probably very motivated.*

First, read the marketplace. Obviously, you are going to stay close to or even exceed the asking price if there is a lot of competition among buyers. Your agent may tell you there are others ready to make a full-price offer, but it's really up to you to read that statement as a fact or as sales talk.

Be aware that experts consider a 5 percent difference in property valuations too close to call. A $200,000 property could be valued at $190,000 or $210,000 and still be within the margin of accuracy. In the typical market (not hot nor depressed), you often can get a seller to accept an offer that is 5 percent lower than the asking price. A 10 percent reduction is common when the property is obviously overpriced or when the seller *must* sell within a short period. Your agent will expect to defend any price cut of 10 percent or more with data from recent sales of comparable properties.

Insider's Tip

Knowing how long a home has been on the market can be useful when negotiating price. Newer listings typically expect something near the listed price, while those that are about to expire may be more open to a lower offer. You can ask the age of a specific listing, though the agent may not tell you. Also, you may not know if the home has been relisted recently. Typically, listings are for 90 days, though some sellers will only sign for 60 and, in slower markets, some brokers want 120-day listings. Listings for new condos and town houses are often for 180 days or longer.

Also think of the price in terms of monthly payment. For example, $1,000 financed at 5.5 percent interest for thirty years is $5.68 a month. The same for fifteen years is $8.17. So a $10,000 price reduction means a savings of about $57 to $82 a month. On the one hand, it's a good savings—and on the other a small amount compared to not getting the home you want. In many marketplaces, the $10,000 will be gained back in appreciation in a year or less.

In a typical marketplace, you can do better by offering something near the asking price and getting other valuable concessions. You may need more time to sell your existing home, you may need to move into the new home quickly, you may want the seller to leave specific personal property (range, refrigerator, shelving, what have you), or you may ask the seller to take a short-term second mortgage for the property. Remember, it's about compromise. Your agent will be more willing to help you include contingencies than to lower the asking price. Use your agent's knowledge and negotiating skills to your advantage.

Insider's Tip

If you are making an offer on a home subject to the sale of your existing home, make sure your agents communicate with each other. Your selling agent needs to know if you are buying another home, and your buying agent needs to answer questions that sellers will have about your ability to buy. You can be the go-between, but it's often more efficient to have the two agents talk directly. A conference call is even better.

To learn even more about the home-buying process, ask your agent to describe how the offer will be presented. Typically, your agent tells the listing agent that she or he has an offer to present to the seller. Your agent may or may not summarize the terms to the listing agent. If the listing agent feels the terms won't be acceptable, the two agents may discuss how best to present the offer. In most cases, the listing agent introduces your agent to the sellers as a subagent. Then your agent presents the offer's terms. Many agents discuss the positive terms first (including you, the buyer), then the negatives. If the price is a positive and the date of occupancy is a negative, the agent probably will present them in that order. As needed, your agent may describe you, discuss your qualifications for considering the home, and maybe share some of your positive comments about the property. Or the agent may not. Each presentation is a little different. Asking your agent to describe how the offer will be presented gives you the opportunity to provide information that may or may not be used to help sell your offer.

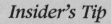

Insider's Tip

What can you do if, too late, you feel that your agent or the seller's agent has misrepresented the property or has conspired against you, the buyer? First, go talk with the broker who hired your salesperson. If necessary, that broker will discuss the problem with the seller's broker, the person ultimately responsible for the transaction. If you still can't get satisfaction, take the issue to the local real estate board and/or an attorney.

Handling Counteroffers

There are three options the seller has when receiving an offer to purchase: Accept it, reject it, or make a counteroffer. For obvious reasons, your agent will work to turn a rejection into a counteroffer. Basically it says that the seller accepts some, but not all, of the terms of your offer, and lists specific terms to replace those that are unacceptable. Your agent and the listing agent will work with the seller to develop terms that you, the buyer, are most likely to accept.

The seller may accept your offered price but make a counteroffer regarding who pays for specific closing costs, how long until financing must be obtained, or other conditions. Every term in your offer is one that can be rejected and countered, though agents will remind the seller that the buyer doesn't have to accept any of them, thus ending the deal.

Pitfall

Beware of any agent, yours or the seller's, who wants any part of the deal verbal rather than in writing. Real estate law requires that all terms of a property transaction be in writing and signed by all relevant parties. No side deals.

The counteroffer will be in writing on a form similar to the RPA. In fact, in many states, a minor counteroffer such as a price change can be made on the RPA and initialed. Other states require a separate counteroffer form for *any* change.

How should you handle a counteroffer? Without emotion. Don't get mad. If it is totally unacceptable, reject it or allow it to expire without acceptance. The seller may have second thoughts in a few days and ask you (through your agent) to make a new offer under specified terms. If most of the terms of the counter are acceptable, you can make a counter to the counteroffer. Just remember that the seller can refuse to consider your counter-counter and the deal is dead.

Insider's Tip

How long should you give the seller to consider your offer to purchase? Your agent can advise you regarding special circumstances (divorce, estate, out-of-town seller) that require more time, but most RPAs are written to expire within one to three days.

Accepting Your Offer

What if the sellers decide they can live with the terms of your offer—or you decide you can live with the terms of the seller's counteroffer? Then the seller signs the RPA (and you sign any counteroffers), and the transaction begins. I'll cover closing the transaction in the next chapter. Meantime, congratulations!

Let me warn you about a prevalent disease called *buyer's remorse*. It begins with the sensation that you've made an irrevocable decision that will dramatically change the course of your life and that of the free world! Fortunately, it's a phantom disease. If you've done your homework, hired a competent agent, and taken precautions along the way, your decision is more than likely a good one. It may not feel that way, especially when a friend says, "You should have used my agent; she wouldn't let you pay that much for it!" or, "This is a really bad time to buy a home. You're going to get stuck!" Not really friends, are they? Ignore them. You have learned how the real estate market works, how to get the best from it, and how to hire a professional real estate agent who will cover your back. You're a smart buyer.

Summary

Making an offer to buy a home is scary. Fortunately, you know what you're doing. You know what making an offer to purchase is all about, how to include valuable conditions, how to help your agent make the offer and handle counteroffers. Finally, you've seen that buying isn't really that scary—with good advice and a good agent. Again, congratulations!

CHAPTER 11

Getting to Closing

*A*nxious? You've selected and purchased a house or apartment that fits your needs, and you probably want to get moved in this weekend. Not so fast! There are some legal things that have to be done and, unless you are paying all cash, some financial hoops to jump through.

This chapter shows you how to get into your new home faster and with fewer problems. Your agent is being paid to help with this process, but there are things you can do as well to keep everyone honest and working hard for you. Let's get started.

Getting into Escrow

In chapter 1, you learned that *escrow* occurs when the seller and buyer hire a neutral third party to handle the transfer of property rights and money between them. The escrow agent or officer can be the title company, the lender, an attorney, or an independent service specializing in escrowing real estate transactions. The escrow agent is in charge of *closing* on the transaction.

Lingo

To close (verb) means to go through a transaction between the seller and buyer transferring ownership of a specific property; it's a process. The *closing* (noun) is the event when sellers and buyers sign final papers to make the ownership transfer happen.

The closing process begins when the real estate agent (if you are using one) delivers the Residential Purchase Agreement (RPA) and earnest money deposit to whomever the seller and buyer agree upon to escrow the transaction. In most cases, sellers and buyers look to their real estate agents to recommend an escrow service. The buyer's agent may suggest the buyer's lender, or the seller's agent will recommend whoever escrowed when the seller purchased the home. As long as everyone agrees, it really doesn't matter.

The earnest money may be in the form of a check from the buyer or an IOU from the buyer payable when the RPA is signed by both seller and buyer. The escrow service uses the RPA as instructions for the transaction. That's why it's very important to have a clear and well-written RPA. The escrow service is looking for the seller's and buyer's instructions on:

➤ Final purchase price and terms.

➤ Legal data (property description, who is selling, and who is buying).

➤ Time period for the close of escrow and inspection or additional earnest money deposit.

➤ Contingencies (financing, inspections, appraisals, and so on).

➤ Who pays for what services.

The escrow service will develop a transaction worksheet from the RPA so it doesn't miss anything. All contingencies must be completed by all parties before the escrow service will simultaneously release title to the buyer and funds to the seller.

To make sure that the seller actually has title to sell the property, a preliminary title report is issued by a local title company. The report is based on a search of public records of the county, such as the tax collector, county recorder, and assessor's office. The report will list any liens, taxes, easements, encumbrances, or title defects on the property found in the search. Because this is what title companies do for a living, a preliminary title search and report should take only a few days.

Who Pays for What

The closing costs are paid based on the RPA and local convention. In many locations, the *seller* typically pays for:

- Real estate commissions.

- Document preparation fees.

- Document transfer taxes.

- Notary fees.

- Payoff of all loans in the seller's name.

- Existing liens, taxes, and judgments currently against the property.

- Pest inspections and any work required by inspections (as limited by the RPA).

- Home warranty policy, if offered.

- Prorated taxes to the date of transfer.

- Any other costs or fees as outlined in the RPA.

In many locations, the *buyer* typically pays for:

- Title insurance premiums.

- Document preparation.

- All or half of the escrow and notary fees.

- Recording fees.

- Loan costs and fees, including down payment.

- Prorated taxes from the date of transfer.

- Inspection fees not paid by the seller.

- Hazard insurance premium from the date of transfer.

All these components are negotiable and not set by law. They also may vary from location to location. As a buyer, you may have your agent negotiate the payment of any or all of these typical fees.

Insider's Tip

How much should you expect to pay for closing costs? Because loan costs are the largest chunk of closing costs, a transaction with a mortgage loan typically has closing costs of about 3 percent of the purchase price ($6,000 on a $200,000 purchase). Closing costs for purchases without loans are as low as 1 percent ($2,000 on a $200,000 house). Remember that you can negotiate to have the seller pay more or less than the buyer's customary closing costs on your behalf. If your current home doesn't sell before you need the proceeds to purchase another home, you may be able to use the equity in your current home to get a short-term loan to close on the new one. Be aware that lenders will be very cautious issuing a loan that exceeds your assets or earning power if you are somehow stuck with two homes. The best advice is to discuss with your current lender, your new lender (if different), and your real estate agent the best method of making the transition.

How Long Until Closing?

Everyone probably wants the transaction to close quickly. The faster the sale is closed and recorded, the faster everyone can move on. So a big question will be, *How long will it take to close on this property?* The answer is: *It depends.* Typical is about sixty days if there is a lender involved.

If the deal requires proceeds from the sale of the buyer's home, the sale will be delayed until that event occurs. It may be ten days if the home is sold and waiting to close or it may be months if no buyers are in sight yet.

Another major contingency that needs to be cleared up before closing is funding. How are you paying for your new home? If you're paying cash and there is no lender, all you need to do is make the funds available to the escrow service. That may mean cashing in CDs, transferring funds from a money market account, or otherwise depositing liquid funds. If the purchase is subject to financing, you need to make an application for the loan, get

The Escrow Process

The typical escrow process includes the following sequence of events:

- Escrow is opened by the agent or lender.

- Earnest money, if any, is deposited with the escrow service, typically within three days.

- Escrow instructions are developed based on the Residential Purchase Agreement, addendums, and any preliminary loan papers.

- The preliminary title search and re-port are ordered from the title service.

- The loan is approved by the lender, as needed.

- New lenders provide the escrow service with loan documents, as needed.

- As required by the lender, proof of hazard insurance on the property is provided by the buyer.

- Holders of all existing liens and judgments issue a demand for payment through escrow at least two weeks before closing.

- The escrow service produces closing documents for signature by the seller, buyer, and all other parties involved in the transaction.

- All parties in the transaction sign documents in front of a notary (typically the escrow officer); at the same time, the buyer may be required to sign the lender's loan papers.

- Deeds and mortgage papers are forwarded by the escrow company to the county recorder for official recording.

- Escrow disburses the funds as instructed by escrow and loan documents to the seller, buyer (refunds), and all agents.

- Your agent calls you to say, "The house is yours!"

- Everyone celebrates!

approval, and get the lender to write the final check. I recommend that you take care of this step earlier in the buying process (chapter 8) to save time at closing. Getting prequalified and prefunded can save you weeks or even months of the closing process.

Keeping Everything Moving

Smaller contingencies and conditions also need to be taken care of before closing. If you've hired a good agent, that agent will take the initiative to help keep everything moving. There are numerous small details that must be managed, resolved, and signed off. The RPA and the escrow instructions list them. The agent or the agent's assistant can keep you apprised of what has been done and what needs to be done. As a double-check, make sure your agent is meeting the deadlines set in the purchase agreement and is communicating with other agents in the transaction. A good agent will probably be on top of every-thing, but it doesn't hurt to verify. Your agent will appreciate the effort. Hey, it's *your* house!

Insider's Tip

Want to know how much closing costs will be? The Real Estate Set-tlement Procedures Act (RESPA) requires that lenders issue a "good faith" (lender's best) estimate of the costs of a loan. Of course, this is only the cost of the *loan,* not other closing costs paid out of escrow. It tells you what the loan itself will probably cost.

Pitfall

Be very careful about exceeding the close-of-escrow date agreed upon in the RPA. Technically, if the date is exceeded by even one day the sale can be annulled. Don't listen to any agent who tells you that the seller has *verbally* agreed to extend the closing date. Remember, there are *no verbal agreements* in real estate. If you believe the closing will not occur by the specified date, ask your agent to get a *written and signed* addendum from the seller extending the date as needed.

Another condition of the sale may be inspection by you and/or a professional housing inspector. Take care of these as early as possible so that, if there is a problem, the property can be reinspected with plenty of time left to close. Make sure you allow time for any needed repairs. Also make sure that any inspection or other conditions are "signed off" or approved in writing as appropriate—and that the escrow service knows about it. Your agent should make sure this happens, but it doesn't hurt to double-check. It's *your* money!

Insider's Tip

Remember that it's really you, the buyer, who holds the keys to the transaction. No one gets paid—seller, lender, agents—until you pay for the property. Use the strength of this position to keep everyone working toward the common goal. If necessary, gently remind them that you found a good home and that you can find another if necessary.

Preclosing

About one week before the scheduled closing event (when everybody sits down to sign papers), most of the components needed to close the transaction will be in place. Loan documents are returned to your lender for final funding, all contingencies are signed off, title insurance is written, and the escrow worksheet is ready for completion. There's nothing left to do but wait for the lender's check, if appropriate.

Lingo

Title insurance is an insurance policy that protects the holder from loss due to defects in a specific property's title. Most mortgage lenders require that the buyer have title insurance on the subject property.

Actually, there is one more thing. You should ask your real estate agent to review the closing papers a few days before closing. The agent can verify that all the instructions on the RPA have been carried out by the escrow service. In addition, an experienced agent can save you some money by catching nickel-and-dime charges that aren't necessary. Catching them on the day of closing can delay things, so many people let them slide. Your agent can catch them now and possibly save you some money. You should also find out the amount of the cashier's check you need to bring with you when signing closing papers. The check will include the balance of the down payment and all closing costs.

Insider's Tip

Uncomfortable with signing all these papers without a lawyer? No problem. At least a week or two in advance, notify your agent and the escrow service that you want your attorney to look over all papers before you sign them. It may delay the process slightly, but it can help you sleep better at night. If the transaction is complex anyway, you may prefer to hire a real estate attorney to handle the escrow instead of an escrow service. Just remember that the attorney will add clauses to protect him- or herself as well.

Some of the overcharges are simply errors and oversights. Yes, even escrow services can make mathematical mistakes or put something into the wrong column. These can cost you hundreds or even thousands of dollars unless caught. In addition, fees can add up in unnecessary and expensive courier charges. An overnight courier charge may be made when there is no hurry or when the offices are next to each other. Hey, it may be just $50 or $100, but it's all money. Use it to splurge on a celebration dinner.

Closing

Get your ink pens out! You're going to need them to sign all the papers that will be presented to you at the closing. There will be transfer documents, loan documents (if not previously signed), recording documents that go to the courthouse, and various documents developed by lawyers to protect the agents, escrow, and other transaction service providers.

This book shows you how to make it a no-surprises closing by knowing what's coming and being ready for it. But problems can still occur up to the moment when all the papers are fully signed. The seller can get sick or injured—or cold feet. A delivery service strike can hold up paperwork. A natural disaster can delay all transactions in your area. That's why it's important to try *not* to sign closing papers on the last day you can. Give yourself at least a week of time between closing and the last date of closing allowed in the RPA. One bump in a complex transaction can make it all fall apart, wasting everyone's time and money. Leave some room at the closing table for Murphy's Law!

Moving Out, In, and On

Can you move in the day you sign closing papers? Probably not, unless you have a written agreement with the seller to do so—and the seller has already moved out. Instead, you must wait at least for the official recording of the transfer of title. The escrow service forwards all the legal documents to the county recorder to be officially recorded. Until this happens and funds are disbursed, technically, the transaction isn't complete.

Once you've received notice that the transaction is officially recorded and proceeds are disbursed by the escrow service, you can move into your new property *based on the terms of the RPA*. In many cases, your occupancy can officially start at the closing of escrow. The sellers, however, may have included a clause in the RPA that they have ten, twenty, or any other number of days to vacate so you can move in. If so, there will probably be a per-day rental fee they must pay, already spelled out in the RPA. Alternatively, your agent may have negotiated an early-occupancy agreement whereby you are able to legally move in *as renters* before the official closing date. You, too, will probably pay a per-day rental fee. Early and late occupancies can get tricky, which is where a good real estate agent can be very useful.

How do you coordinate moving services or truck rental? With the help of your real estate agent. The agent's experience and contacts can be useful when you're trying to schedule one mover to clear out the seller's stuff and another to replace it with yours. Remember, though, that this coordination service is a courtesy to you and not required by the agent's agreement with the seller or with you. It's done primarily because the agent wants to impress you and earn referrals and future business.

Of course, there's more to moving in than carrying furniture in the front door. There's getting utilities turned on or transferred, getting any children settled into schools, finding medical and other service providers if you're in a new neighborhood, and many other tasks. If you've selected a professional real estate agent, your job may be made much easier by the agent or the agent's assistant, who can help you get settled in.

Summary

As you can see, the closing process is where a good agent shines. The agent takes care of the paperwork, oversees the escrow service, coordinates with lenders and inspectors, and keeps everything moving toward title transfer—and the agent's payday. A good agent earns every dollar of his or her fees—and earns your referral. That's what good real estate agents do!

PART THREE

Buying a Home Without an Agent

CHAPTER 12

Building Your Support Team

*Y*ou really don't *need* a real estate agent to help you buy a home or apartment—a fact that most agents won't tell you. So what *do* you need?

Actually, you can do it all yourself, depending on the type of transaction. You can review the legal documents, pay cash or work directly with lenders, appraise the property's value, inspect it, and even negotiate with the seller to handle the closing process between you. Of course, you may need to expand your knowledge of the law, housing, and other fields before attempting it on your own, but you *can* do it. In this chapter, I'll show you how. I'll also show you how to put together a team of professionals who will help you get the home you want without a real estate agent.

Hiring the Team

Whom do you need on your team? The answer depends on what you are buying, where, how, and what you can handle yourself. If you're experienced with legal documents, have strong negotiating skills, and are paying cash, you may need only one or two more people for your team. Most financed home purchases, however, require at least an attorney, a lender, an appraiser, and an inspector, plus title and escrow services.

Where are you going to find potential team members? As covered in chapter 3, lenders hold the key to buying property that requires financing. And chapter 8 suggests that you get your money first, even before looking at specific properties. So it makes sense to select a lender first. It makes even more sense because a lender can be the key to finding other real estate professionals. Mortgage lenders are the biggest players in most real estate purchases, so they know and can recommend qualified attorneys, appraisers, inspectors, and other service providers. If you find the best lender (not necessarily the one with the lowest rates), you'll find a network of other pros.

Insider's Tip

To learn more about the real estate process, make sure you read part 2 of this book, "Getting the Most from a Real Estate Agent." It will show you what you yourself need to do to replace the agent in a purchasing transaction.

Lender

To start the home-buying process, first interview mortgage lenders in your area. Try the savings bank or credit union you use as well as mortgage companies and brokers that have offices near you. You may find a better deal elsewhere, but you may not get the personal service and the education that you can get with a face-to-face meeting. So make some appointments and start learning.

What do you want to know?

➤ Types of mortgages offered (fixed, ARM, fifteen-year, thirty-year, and so on).

➤ Current interest rates (APR).

➤ Points (prepaid interest) and loan fees.

➤ Credit requirements.

➤ Typical time needed to get funds.

➤ The loan application and approval process.

➤ Tips and suggestions on making the loan process go smoother.

➤ Other professionals they can recommend (attorneys, appraisers, title and escrow, and the like).

Insider's Tip

Make sure the lender you select can give you a written, not just a verbal, loan commitment. Most are good for thirty to sixty days, with extensions possible if nothing has changed on your credit report such as employment or available down payment.

Interview a few lenders and you'll soon determine which is the most professional. They may not have the lowest rates, but often you can bring back a rate from another lender and ask the one you prefer to match it—or at least come close. Working with the best lender will be worth a couple of dollars a month for the next thirty years!

A major advantage to look for is that some lenders have a proven team already set up. They have a staff or preferred real estate attorney, appraisers, inspectors, title service, and escrow service, maybe even under the same roof. This can make your search easier. Remember, however, that the best lender may not have the best attorney on staff. You still may have to shop for other pros on your own.

Insider's Tip

Review chapters 3 and 8 for additional information on how lenders work, where to find them, and how to get the best loan you can.

Attorney

Attorneys are the subject of thousands of jokes, but there also are some good ones out there. Of course, you don't want one who takes whiplash claims and DWI defendants. You want an attorney who specializes—or at least works primarily—in real estate.

Here are some of the sources where you can find real estate attorneys:

➤ Local lenders.

➤ Yellow pages of the telephone book.

➤ Local attorney referral services (listed in the telephone book).

➤ Friends and co-workers.

➤ Escrow and title services.

➤ Real estate offices.

Insider's Tip

If you are concerned about the title (chapter 1) of a specific property, hire a real estate attorney with title experience to perform an *attorney's opinion of title.* You may also need an attorney if you are buying your first property after a bankruptcy, divorce, or other financial problem.

You may not *need* an attorney. You can purchase real estate forms through stationery stores and online that will give you the basic clauses needed for simple transactions. You can, if you wish, have an attorney look over the forms and give you some pointers, saving time and money. Some attorneys' offices even offer forms and minimal advice at a price somewhere between custom forms and preprinted you're-on-your-own forms.

What should you ask attorney candidates?

➤ *What is your training and experience specifically with residential real estate?*

➤ *What services do you offer to home buyers?*

➤ *What are your rates and how do they compare with those of other real estate attorneys in the area?*

Many attorneys offer a free initial consultation, typically only a half hour or hour for basic questions. You may get sufficient free advice from this meeting to handle the transaction yourself, although most attorneys won't give away more than necessary to sell you on their service.

Insider's Tip

A real estate attorney also can be useful if you are purchasing property in a location in which you are unfamiliar and need representation. Not as inexpensive as hiring a real estate agent, an attorney can better represent your rights and even purchase property on your behalf.

Appraiser

An appraiser is someone hired to estimate the value of real property. Of course, nearly anyone can do that, but the accuracy may be off. And when you're working with hundreds of thousands of dollars, a 20 percent margin for error is too big. You want an appraisal that the lender will accept as legitimate. Most lenders have a list of approved appraisers. If you aren't using a lender, you can ask other members of your team for recommendations.

Many lenders require appraisals done by a Certified Residential Appraiser. This person has both training and experience in appraising residential properties for value. In most states, certification requires some college, often two years' worth, specific training in appraisal, field experience, and passing tests.

Pitfall

Not all appraisers are certified; nor are they even qualified. Many states don't have licensing requirements for appraisers as they do for real estate agents. It's up to lenders or consumers to make sure they are hiring a qualified appraiser. Unfortunately, some lenders don't really care and will hire anyone who can spell *appraisal*. The problem comes when you want to sell your property and it isn't worth anything like what the appraisal said.

Inspectors

Sellers typically hire the cheapest inspector. You, the buyer, should want the *best*. You want someone who is thorough and accurate. Still, unless you specify the inspector in your offer to purchase, the seller probably will select whoever is cheapest and least likely to find problems. You can hire your own inspector as well, but it's easier and less expensive if the seller and buyer can agree on the inspector early on.

What kind of inspector? Most homes should be inspected for two things: safety and pests. The safety inspection is also known as the building inspection. It makes sure that the home was built and remodeled according to local building codes, and that any safety issues are identified. Pest inspection checks to see if there is or will soon be damage caused by pests such as carpenter ants, rodents, and other critters as well as mold, dry rot, and water damage.

How can you find a qualified inspector or two? Again, ask the lender. Better, ask a few lenders. Some aren't as careful about hiring the best inspector as others are. If you get a consensus that XYZ Inspection Services can do a full inspection to find any hidden problems, that's who you use.

Pitfall

Be specific when asking for an inspection. You want both a pest inspection and a building inspection. "Yes, it's been inspected" doesn't tell you which—or what the inspectors found. Ask for a copy of *all* inspection reports. Make sure your offer to purchase includes a clause requiring both inspections or a combined inspection *and* specifies your recourse if the property fails inspection.

Title

In most locations, you may only have one or two choices of local title insurers with good rates. If the seller pays for title insurance, you may not have much say. Still, many lenders that work daily with title companies have a preference. One company may offer faster turnaround, boast fewer errors, or have a better reputation for quality than others. Ask your lender if it has a preference and suggest this to the seller as you write up the agreement. Most sellers don't care, but your friend the lender may.

Insider's Tip

Want to know who owns a specific parcel and other facts of public record? Many title companies offer a concise title report free or at a small charge as a promotion to earn new business. I'll tell you how to use this title report to your advantage in chapter 15.

Escrow

Escrow companies are often overlooked because they are built into the lender or the title company. A good escrow service, however, can make your purchase much easier. You, the buyer, have a say in which escrow service is chosen to hold and coordinate funds, so find out what you can about local escrow services. You're looking for experience and, more important, accuracy. Lenders *may* tell you whether a specific escrow service has fewer errors in closing papers than others. You certainly don't want someone on your team who makes costly mistakes.

If there is no real estate agent, you or the seller (or both) will be delivering the purchase agreement to the escrow service. It's a good idea to talk with an escrow officer first to make sure you know what she or he needs to open an escrow account.

Lingo

An *escrow account* or *trust account* is a separate account into which funds are deposited and withdrawn for a specific real estate transaction, never commingled with business or other transaction funds.

Summary

Buying real estate is typically a team effort. You can hire some or all of the expertise you need. Alternatively, you can educate yourself and tackle more of it—or keep your team members honest.

CHAPTER 13

Finding Property for Sale

*A*bout one in four residences for sale is offered directly by the seller rather than through a real estate agent. That's millions of houses and apartments each year that are sold without an agent. Smart buyers find smart sellers and strike a deal.

This chapter offers proven methods and tips on finding property without an agent. You'll learn where to look, what to ask, how to avoid traps and pitfalls, and how to work around renters. Following chapters will show you how to buy from builders, how to make an offer, and how to manage a successful transaction—and save money!

What Are You Looking For?

Pull out your Buyer's Notebook (chapter 4) to review what you're looking for. You are now the agent—the one who does the legwork searching for the right home for you, the client. The reward is the potential for saving all or most of the commission the seller would pay—typically $12,000 on a $200,000 house.

As a refresher, here are the steps to determining what you want in your next home:

➤ Identify your needs.

➤ Study the marketplace.

➤ Select and learn the neighborhood.

➤ Eliminate properties that obviously don't match.

➤ Further research the properties that match your needs.

➤ Make the best decision you can.

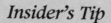

Insider's Tip

Many neighborhoods have homeowner associations (HAs), intended to keep out the riffraff. Most condos and town houses have them. Some HAs strictly enforce their rules, while others are quite lax. Make sure you find out how the HA in your chosen neighborhood is set up and how active it is in enforcement. Of course, once you move in you can help guide it toward balanced policies.

As your own agent, you need to consider as many properties as you can. For every property that a good agent brings you, he or she probably has considered ten. That's your job now: looking for candidate properties and matching them to your needs.

Insider's Tip

To efficiently find the home you're looking for, know your needs, prioritize your wants, consider all options, and educate yourself about the local real estate market.

Where Should You Look?

The first place to start looking for your next property is in the neighborhood you've selected (chapter 4). This time, however, you are looking for FSBOs (*fizz-bos*), For-Sale-By-Owners. You're looking for signs erected by the owners indicating that their property is for sale directly from the seller.

Another place to look is at the tax collector's office. Some homes are foreclosed on due to delinquent taxes. Some time spent on researching properties near foreclosure can help you find motivated sellers!

Use your Buyer's Notebook to keep track of the numerous houses and apartments you will consider over the next few weeks. You can group them by neighborhood, street, section of town, asking price, or anything else that helps you keep them from running together in your mind. Professional real estate agents typically keep notes by price and neighborhood.

In addition to driving around in preferred neighborhoods, you can find FSBOs in local newspapers. Some regions of the country and even parts of town have more FSBOs than others. The area you select may have very few—or the number may approach 50 percent of available properties. Daily and weekly newspapers and shopper papers are a good place to find them.

Insider's Tip

Some FSBOs put up a sign, place an ad, and, if nothing happens, drop the ad after a month or two. That means the only way you'll know that their homes are for sale is to see the sign in the front yard.

Besides driving and reading, you may find FSBOs on the Internet. If you're not familiar with online research and shopping, find a relative or friend who is and ask for help in your search. Some of the online addresses you can try include:

- ➤ realestate.yahoo.com
- ➤ homeadvisor.com
- ➤ ired.com
- ➤ homes.com
- ➤ homeseekers.com
- ➤ homestore.com

> homefair.com

> greathomes.org

Also, you can use one of the major search engines (google.com, yahoo.com) to find homes for sale in your city, town, or neighborhood. In communities that are built around high technology, you may find hundreds of FSBOs online. Can you safely research online? Typically, yes. You're not actually buying the house online, plunking down thousands of dollars. Instead you are researching what is available.

Insider's Tip

One advantage to shopping for housing online is that many sites include digital photos of the exterior and interior. Some even have video or 360-degree views. Many also have links to preferred financing sources. The Internet is just a tool; in the hands of a smart seller who knows marketing, it can be a great tool for you, the buyer.

Finding Flowers Among the Weeds

Of course, not all potential homes are obviously for sale. Many sellers who aren't in a hurry prefer to use word-of-mouth advertising to promote their properties. Others are considering selling, but aren't sure enough to put the sign up quite yet.

You can find budding properties the same way that smart real estate agents do: by farming. You can harvest properties within a specific geographic area as they become ready. Agents know this. They also know that by carefully planting and cultivating, they can find willing sellers. Here are some suggestions:

> Print up business cards with your specific housing needs and how to contact you, then pass them to anyone you meet.

> Farm any of your social groups that may have members in the chosen neighborhood: church, synagogue, mosque,

ashram, PTA, co-workers, clubs, what have you. Let people know what you're looking for and where.

Insider's Tip

Need a neighborhood map to plan your farm? You often can buy one at the city or county courthouse that has jurisdiction over the neighborhood. Buy the map in a handy size, then get a printout, if available, of all the property owners within the area. Due to privacy laws, you may not be able to purchase these through the courthouse, but many mailing services have them, developed from the telephone directory.

> ➤ Print and mail postcards to all residents of the chosen neighborhood describing your search for a home in the area and asking that they call you if theirs is for sale. A local mailing service can get you the addresses and even label and mail the cards for you.

> ➤ Print and place flyers at commercial gathering points in your chosen neighborhood, such as store bulletin boards, restaurants, Laundromats, and other places.

Of course, farming takes more time than calling up FSBO ads. Still, if you have the time to cultivate potential sellers you may find them very agreeable to reducing their price by the $10,000 to $20,000 they will save by not using a real estate agent.

Insider's Tip

Remember that you don't have to live nearby to farm a neighborhood. Even from thousands of miles away, you can place Want-to-Buy ads and mail postcards for a neighborhood in which you want to live.

Buying a Foreclosure

You may have heard that buying a foreclosure is the best way to save money on your next home. It *can* be. You must, however, know how foreclosures work; the right home must be available; and you must be ready to finance it or pay cash. Here's Foreclosure 101.

A *foreclosure* is the forced sale of a piece of real estate to pay a debt. It occurs when the property owner gives up the right to redeem it after the loan against the property goes into default. A foreclosure sale is then held. Depending on the type of foreclosure, the sale is held by the courts or by a trustee such as the lender.

Lingo

Foreclosure is the termination of a mortgagee's right of redemption. Some states allow a statutory right of redemption, however, which allows the previous owner to redeem the property as much as one year after it has been sold under foreclosure.

So the best place to look for information on foreclosures is court records and lender foreclosure departments. Most foreclosures require that notices be published. You may not find such notices in your local newspaper, though; they may be published in a local, state, or regional publication made up entirely of public notices. In addition, there are numerous Web sites that publish foreclosure notices and information.

Pitfall

Foreclosure notices typically are public record. That means you don't have to pay to see them. Be wary of any company that attempts to sell you foreclosure information for any amount beyond a small service fee.

You will also hear about preforeclosure sales. These often are conducted by firms that specialize in working with sellers who are in default on a mortgage, but actual foreclosure hasn't occurred. The advantage is that you may get a good deal on a property at below market value. Of course, there is an agent involved, so some of the savings will be lost to fees.

Residential properties can be sold at auction as well. In most cases, the auction is held because the seller needs to get out from under the debt and can't wait for the marketplace to find a buyer. Check local telephone books for real estate auction services. Also, ask county appraiser and tax offices if they know of any auction services that work in the area you're searching.

If you are online, check out foreclosure.com, all-foreclosure.com, and hud.gov. Also use a search engine to find foreclosure and preforeclosure notification services for your area.

What *Not* to Buy

Professional real estate agents know what to steer you away from. If you are your own agent, you may not recognize what *not* to buy. I'll share some with you. *Don't buy:*

➤ Homes that need more repair than you can do.

➤ Homes that need more repair than you can hire to be done.

➤ Condos and town houses that have management or legal problems.

➤ Life estate title (chapter 1), unless you understand how it works and have good legal advice.

➤ Homes that lenders wouldn't loan on.

➤ Houses or apartments from relatives or friends—unless you're willing for it to potentially damage your relationship.

➤ Residential properties that are too good to be true (dollar-down foreclosures and the like).

➤ Homes offered by sellers who push too hard or refuse to disclose facts of condition, title, prior damage and repair, or potential hazards (sinkholes, slides, and so forth).

➤ Homes that might be a good investment but don't fit your needs or tastes.

Insider's Tip

Many, but not all, states mandate lemon laws and cooling-off periods after a major sale is made. The point is that many buyers make decisions based on excessive emotion, frustration, or coercion. It's common enough that there are laws allowing for it. Don't buy for the wrong reasons.

You can probably add further to this list of what *not* to buy. There may be a local neighborhood or group of homes in which you should not buy due to geological or social problems. Or you may want to avoid a specific home builder's units because of excessive complaints. These are things a good agent will know about but you may not, so you must educate yourself.

Insider's Tip

Be careful of buying a "white elephant," a home that is too expensive to maintain or heat. If you're concerned about heating or cooling bills for a specific house or apartment, make sure you include a contingency or condition that requires an energy audit and limits the average energy bill. Also beware houses that will require more ongoing maintenance than you want to or can afford to provide. Energy and maintenance dollars have the same value as mortgage dollars.

Avoiding Common Problems

Buyers working through mediocre agents are subject to misinformation or withheld information. If you are your own agent, you are subject to lack of information. You may not have considered an important element of selecting a house—until you own it! This book and especially this part are written to help you avoid many of the common mistakes that home buyers face. In addition, here are some general tips on buying your next home without an agent.

➤ Don't buy more than you realistically need. Plan for family expansion, of course, but don't purchase a home that is well out of your budget because it is a good deal. It may wind up as someone else's foreclosure bargain.

➤ Don't buy more than you can afford *next year.* If you know that your job will end soon and prospects for a better one aren't strong, don't hope that you'll find something. Be as sure as you can.

➤ Don't believe everything you hear. Verify anything the seller or others not members of your support team (chapter 12) tell you. And it's a good idea to verify their facts as well. It's *your* money.

Insider's Tip

How can you verify facts? Ask yourself, *Who else would know this fact?* If it regards the property size or taxes, ask the county assessor. If it's about the local marketplace, ask two or three agents or lenders for verification. If it concerns the condition of the property, hire an inspector.

➤ Beware houses and apartments that have had recent cosmetic changes. A smart seller will paint as needed and enjoy it rather than wait until just before it's offered for sale—unless the seller is trying to cover something.

➤ Don't assume that all sellers are relatively inexperienced. Some are dealers who buy and sell homes for a living. Some were previously real estate agents. What may look like a good solution could be a well-hidden problem.

Working Around Renters

Because about one-third of the population lives in rental property, chances are that some of the housing you will be considering may have renters. Renters have tenant rights. What rights they have are spelled out in state laws. Typically, however, they have the right to at least twenty-four hours' notice before the property they occupy is shown to buyers, as well as the right to an adequate notice of vacancy before property ownership is transferred. Renters also must allow inspectors to check the property as needed with adequate notice.

Frankly, tenants can be helpful or an encumbrance when you are viewing properties. Some tenants will tell you exactly what's right and wrong with the property, based on their experience. Others will make it difficult to even inspect the property. As you deal with tenants, consider their motives. Some are angry because they soon may be evicted. Some are glad to be helpful—especially if they can get back at the current seller.

Insider's Tip

Don't know what rights renters have in your state? Check with a county or state attorney's office. Specifically, you want to know what rights they have regarding the showing and inspection of property in which they live.

The basic rule is to respect the time and privacy of renters. Remember, however, that a renter who is unreasonable about showing the property should be reported to the seller. It may be that the property is best vacated before offering it for sale.

Summary

You can find property for sale without a real estate agent. Once you've summarized what you're looking for, start seeking FSBOs in neighborhoods, publications, and public records. If you have the time, begin "farming" your favorite neighbor-hoods. Find and consider foreclosures and tax sales. Just remember to be smart and cautious. Someone with more experience will gladly give you expertise in exchange for your money.

CHAPTER 14

Buying from Builders

What if you don't find the home you want? Or what if the house or apartment is offered directly by the builder? How can you buy from builders and make sure you get your money's worth?

These are all good questions. You recognize that buying from a builder is different from buying through an agent or from FSBOs. For one thing, builders are often businesspeople first and can take advantage of buyers who aren't savvy as to how they work. As a general contractor myself, I'll give you some inside information you can use if you're buying from builders.

Advantages and Disadvantages

There are many advantages to buying directly from the house or apartment builder. First, you're getting something new rather than something other people have lived in. It also means that you're getting the latest in construction methods and building code requirements. Another advantage is that you can meet, interview, and learn from the builder—not easily done when the home is ten years or more old. If you buy before the home is actually finished, you may be able to customize it somewhat, at least getting the colors you want. Or you can see how the builder works and possibly have the contractor build a more custom home for you.

Of course, there are disadvantages to buying from a builder. Because builders are businesspeople with thousands or even millions of dollars tied up, they tend to be more difficult to negotiate with. In addition, many builders work with a large bank to handle their day-to-day cash needs, and banks typically aren't very flexible. You may get a 5 or even 10 percent reduction in the price of a used home, but you probably can't get much of a reduction on a new home—unless the bank is forcing the builder to sell units.

Insider's Tip

Want to know who the largest residential home builders are in the area? Ask the largest building materials suppliers. Even if a builder isn't its primary customer, the supplier will know who the major players are.

Insider's Tip

Are new homes a better buy than used homes? In some markets, yes. If there is a shortage of new homes in an area, the prices tend to be higher than comparable used housing. To match apples to apples, divide the asking prices of comparable new and used homes by the homes' square footage to come up with a *per-square-foot* (PSF) price for comparing the two types. If the homes are comparable but the lots aren't (larger, smaller, no landscaping), guess or ask the value of the lots and subtract this from the asking prices before calculating PSF. Alternatively, you can ask a local appraiser for typical PSF prices for new and used homes in the area you are shopping.

Understanding the advantages and disadvantages of buying from builders gives you an edge. Remember (chapter 2), it's really a buyer's market. Unless there is great demand for a specific builder's homes or they are in a hot location and subject to competition from other buyers, you have negotiating power. And even if you are competing with other buyers, you can get the best deal by knowing how builders work.

About Building Contractors

Building contractors are licensed by the state, which means they at least have years of experience in the building trade and have passed standardized tests on business, law, and the construction trades. There are also bonding and insurance requirements. Still, don't expect that these hoops keep out all the riffraff. Like real estate agents, there are good builders, mediocre ones, and unscrupulous ones.

Builders who construct residential houses and apartments are "general building contractors" who serve as the construction manager, overseeing specialized trade contractors, called subcontractors or subs. Trades include concrete, framing, plumbing, electrical, drywall, painting, and HVAC (heating, ventilation, and air-conditioning). It's the general who hires, oversees, inspects, and pays the subs.

Actually it's often a lender who pays for everything. The builder gets a construction loan from the lender and uses it to pay for the land, materials, architect, and subs as needed. There are various stages to construction, and as each stage is completed the lender writes a check to the general to pay subs and suppliers. Why is this point important to you, the buyer? Because anyone who supplies material or labor toward construction can place a lien against the property. When title is researched, all recorded liens will show up and must be resolved in order for the builder to offer clear title. The title company won't offer title insurance unless there is a clean title (all liens are paid off) at the close of escrow.

Lingo

A *lien* is a claim against the title of a property. A mortgage is a general lien. Subcontractors can file a mechanic's lien. Someone suing the builder attempts to file a judgment lien. A lien stays with the title until it is paid off or otherwise cleared in the courts.

As you can imagine, there are various types of builders. Some specialize in single-family residential (SFR) houses, while others build condominiums, cooperative apartments, or town houses. Some contractors build custom homes, others buy a lot and build a house hoping to find a buyer for it, and still other builders work in land developments. A land developer buys and chops up a large parcel of land into smaller parcels, making sure that each lot will have needed services (electrical, water, sewer, telephone, and so forth). A builder can be a land developer, the sole contractor in someone else's development, or even one of many independent contractors within a new development. So the "builder" can be anyone from a small general contractor with one lot and one home plan to a corporation with numerous general contractors on staff, a large land development, and extensive financing.

The way you buy your new home somewhat depends on what type and size of builder you are purchasing from. That's because some builders prefer to sell their homes themselves one at a time, while others have on-staff sales teams or commissioned brokers who sell new and used homes. The actual purchasing process is about the same for all: find, agree, handle contingencies, close. Still, buying a condo or co-op requires different paperwork than buying an SFR. Ownership is different. In addition, larger developers and builders tend to have their own paperwork already drawn up, take it or leave it. So you want to know what you're taking before you sign.

Buying from Spec Builders

Some general contractors make a relatively good living by building two to four homes a year on speculation, with no specific buyer in mind. They have purchased lots or options on lots for a few years in advance, have a friendly lender, have subcontractors and suppliers they can rely on, and can make about 15 to 20 percent gross profit on each house or apartment they build. So they build. Along the way someone hears about them, looks at one of the homes, and buys it. No agent. In tougher markets, the builder may sign a nonexclusive listing (the builder can use other agents and even sell the house her- or himself).

Insider's Tip

If there is an agent involved in the transaction, does the buyer indirectly pay a commission? Of course! But an exclusive agent commission for selling new homes is typically lower than one for used homes. It can be 2 to 5 percent. Alternatively, some builders keep salaried agents on staff to sell their homes. In either case, there is a sales cost that eventually is passed on to the buyer.

Good spec builders offer relatively good pricing on a new home. Most have two or three stock home plans they use, or have a few variations on a single home plan. They don't have to pay architect fees for each new house or apartment, saving money. In addition, the design was probably developed with building economy in mind. This means using modular construction that cuts costs, buying materials in quantity, and making construction more efficient. It doesn't necessarily mean cutting corners. In fact, building the same house over and over can make each unit a little better and less expensive to the builder.

So if you choose to buy a spec home, don't expect custom construction. You're not paying for it. Do expect pricing with little budge in it and more flexible financing than you may otherwise get from a lender. It may be possible to turn the construction loan into a mortgage loan, with fewer fees and less paperwork than buying a used home. The builder's relationship with the lender is important. You may get a brand-new home on better terms than a comparable used home. Sometimes the builder acts as the lender. This can be a great source of income for the builder.

Working with Custom Builders

Custom builders, as you can imagine, work a little differently. In many cases, *you* bring the home plan and hire the builder to make it happen. Alternatively, the custom builder can work with you and an architect to develop a plan that works.

Insider's Tip

Some spec builders also do custom construction, and vice versa. Don't ask a low-end spec home builder to construct your uniquely designed custom home, though: The contractor may not have the skills and subcontractors to do the job you want.

Custom builders are paid in various ways. Because all plans in a custom home are subject to change, however, they often prefer to work on a cost-plus contract. That is, the contractor gets a fee based on a percentage of whatever you spend on construction. Fees vary from 15 to 25 percent of the total construction costs to cover the contractor's skills and experience managing construction. If you decide to add an indoor swimming pool, the contractor says, "Fine!" The contractor may also get a referral discount or fee from subcontractors and suppliers, but only if you, the buyer, know about it. If you go the custom route, make sure an attorney reviews all the contracts before you sign.

In addition, if you have a custom home built you will probably be the one who secures the construction loan, not the contractor. The lender, however, will require that a licensed general contractor be in charge of the project so it gets built to codes and on time.

Insider's Tip

Want to find a custom builder? Start by looking at new-home construction in your chosen area, watching for signs that indicate who is building what. You can also check with the local building department for information on the builder of specific homes you like, for sale or not. If you know someone in the local building trade, ask for recommendations and referrals to custom contractors.

Negotiating with a Builder

Negotiating prices and terms with a builder is different than with a FSBO or through an agent. Most builders work with specific profit margins in mind and cannot easily cut their price—unless the local housing market is deflated. In that case, the lender may participate in reducing the price to move the loan from a short-term construction loan to a long-term first mortgage. Lenders who work with contractors typically work on smaller margins as well, so there may be relatively little flexibility in the sale price.

Terms are another matter. You may be able to get a builder to add some trim, paint or repaint a room or two, or even upgrade carpeting (before it is installed) with cooperative negotiation. In addition, the builder may have clout with the lender to reduce your closing costs or even allow you some flexibility in the credit requirements.

Some builders are speculators as well. That is, they finance their own homes with no outside lender and can sell to you on a contract basis. Most of these contracts have a two- to five-year cash-out, meaning you have to refinance with a traditional lender and pay off the seller/builder. Meantime, you make payments directly to the builder. These deals are especially good for first-time home buyers who may not qualify for traditional lending. The seller doesn't have to answer to a loan department—he or she *is* the loan department. The builder will require that a loan application be completed and will rely heavily on the credit report.

Insider's Tip

You may find used homes that have been remodeled by a contractor and offered for sale under contract terms. They are popular with people trying to get into their first home or trying to buy a home after they have had major credit problems. Buying and paying on such a home gets them into a home and helps them start building a credit rating. Our first home was such a property.

Closing on a New Home

What is required for closing on the sale of a new home? Getting clear title can be either easy or very difficult. It's easy if the builder has managed the project well and paid everyone's bills when due (no liens). If the underlying property was clearly subdivided and sold, the land's title should be okay. If there have been financial problems with the land developer, builder, or other participants, however, it could be a legal mess trying to get clear title to your new home.

Fortunately, that's what a title search and title insurance are all about. You can get a preliminary title search done on the vacant land and check with the lender to determine whether clear title will be a problem. The lender doesn't want cloudy title, either.

Closing will probably be through the lender's or the title company's escrow department. That makes the process easier. Make sure you are represented, though. You don't have a real estate agent to watch out for you, so consider hiring a real estate attorney to check everything over. Just make sure there is no conflict of interest, because the attorney may be hired by the builder or lender. Get your own attorney.

Insider's Tip

How long does it take to close on the sale of a new home? It can be done in days! Larger subdivision builders with spec homes standing by are anxious to transfer ownership and clear their construction loan off the books. So they may have all the closing papers needed awaiting a buyer. If you are prequalified for the loan (chapters 3 and 8), you may be able to close and move in within ten days! It's a great option if you need to find a home fast because the moving van is on the way.

Summary

Don't be afraid to buy from builders. In fact, they can make the buying process easier than it is through an agent or on your own. You can buy a spec house or build your custom home working directly with the builder and saving much of the sales fees. Just make sure you know how builders operate and have an attorney nearby to help you through the legal papers and title process.

CHAPTER 15

Doing Your Own Homework

*I*n school, there's often a temptation to have someone else do a difficult homework assignment for you. Maybe it's math, English, or science. Of course, we know that we don't learn as much that way and that we may not get the best grade, but life's just too darn busy to get that assignment in. There are parties to attend!

Buying real estate can be like that. We're smart enough to do the home-buying homework (title, inspection, appraisal), but it's easier to hire someone else to do it. Unfortunately, you may not be getting what you paid for. That's why this chapter shows you how to do your own homework once you've found the home of your dreams. It will cover how to find info about specific properties, what to look for when inspecting a house or apartment yourself, and how to appraise the value of the home you're buying. As in school, you'll get more value if you do your own homework.

Checking Public Records

Because real estate law requires transactions to be in writing—lots of writing—there is an extensive amount of information on record about every parcel of land in your area. Not all papers get recorded and stored at the courthouse, but enough of them are there to tell you a lot about the properties you are interested in buying. Best of all, viewing these documents is free.

The place to start your search for real estate information is the recorder's office. What it's actually called and where it is located depends on local factors. It may be in a county or parish building, a city or township office, or it may be in an office at the state level. In most locations, all public records relating to real property are held by the county recorder. This includes information on who owns what. Besides basic property information, the mortgage papers, if any, are filed with the recorder. This is where the question of who owns what—title—is answered.

In addition, the same county, parish, or city office building may have a property tax collector's office. Some locations combine it with the recorder's office. If property tax is paid to the city, it may have public tax records as well. The tax records include information about the property to help the tax assessor determine the value of all property in the jurisdiction. It will include details such as the physical size of the land, the size of any structures on the land, what services (sewer, water, electricity, gas) are provided to the property, when it was built, when it was modified, and an estimate of tax value.

Insider's Tip

Tax value is not the same as market value. Market value may fluctuate every year or even faster, but the tax assessors may inspect the property only every two years or more. In between, the assessor will watch public records for property sales and adjust the tax records accordingly. The tax bill on the home you buy may jump dramatically once you buy it. To find out, call your local property tax department and ask how and when properties are appraised for taxes.

Other offices of public record can give you additional information about a specific parcel and the structures on it. The jurisdiction's building department, for example, may have information on the construction of the home. Depending on state and local law, you may or may not be able to see it. It may be in their records, but not *public* record. Even so, the seller may be able to get and share the information with you. Find out how the local building department works.

In many locations, the various departments have made things simpler for buyers, sellers, and builders by including all these records in a single location, typically called a One-Stop. It's where citizens can check on property title, get a building permit for a fence, and ask about property taxes for a specific parcel. Handy!

How can you gather specific property information from the recorder and tax collector? By simply asking for it. These offices prefer to use a tax identification number assigned for each parcel in their jurisdiction, such as 100-259-50-02, or they may ask for a legal description like Lot 84, Block 107, Smallville Subdivision. Most offices, however, will get you the information you need based on a physical street address. If it is an apartment or other multiple-unit dwelling, you'll also need the specific unit number.

Insider's Tip

Why go to all the trouble of doing your homework? Because *you*, not a real estate agent, will present your offer to the seller. If you are offering less than the asking price—or you want the seller to choose your offer over others—doing your homework will help you defend the offer. You actually may know more about the property than the seller does. Negotiate from knowledge.

Researching Title

I covered the concept of property title in chapter 1. You learned that title is one of the rights that a property owner gets and can pass along to others with certain restrictions. Of course, the owner can't sell the property to you without the consent of whoever holds the mortgage, if any. You want to make sure that you get clear title to the property when you buy it—and any lender you use will want the same assurance. This means that someone must research the property's title and find out who, including the seller, has rights to the property.

Fortunately, there are specialists in this legal quagmire, called title attorneys. Actually, staff attorneys typically don't get involved in simple title searches; title officers do. And they don't get their hands too dirty, either, because many use title clerks to pull the records together for review by a title officer.

Insider's Tip

Be especially careful when buying title for a condominium, cooperative apartment, or town house. Make sure you fully understand exactly what *you* own as opposed to what others do. You may have title to your apartment but not the hallway, or a buffer zone at the front of your unit but not on other sides. If in doubt, hire a real estate attorney to explain it clearly for you. It's a good investment in peace of mind.

Title clerks used to spend hours in the local courthouse researching title for individual properties. Today, many title clerks do preliminary research using a computer or a microfiche that views photos of records miniaturized on microfilm. Land records may go back decades or even hundreds of years, though the typical title search goes back only one or two owners, making the job easier.

You can do this: You can research title on any property in your area. Unfortunately, you probably can't *certify* title to the satisfaction of a lender. That requires the services of a title officer or title company. The title company also offers insurance saying that if it misses an important exception to the property's title (liens, mineral rights, easements) and you are sued, it will defend the property and pay any judgment. Unless you're a property attorney *and* an insurance agent, you can't certify title for yourself.

Insider's Tip

Want to find out what's on the public record about a specific piece of property you're interested in? Ask a title insurance company for a *preliminary title report*. There may be a charge for it, or the company may give it to you for free if it believes there's a chance you may buy it and use the company's services.

Inspecting a Property

What should you look for when inspecting a house or apartment you may purchase? The answer depends on what you are buying, where it is, how old it is, and how it was built. If the home is new or relatively new, your inspection may be minimal. If it was built fifty years ago, you are going to be busy inspecting all of the components that could cause problems.

Some of these inspections require an expert, such as the pest inspection. You may be able to see some damages caused by termites, ants, fungi, or other pests, but you may miss others unless you're trained to know what to look for—and trained to use the products that get rid of the pests. A lender won't take your word for it that the pests are gone and damage has been repaired.

Insider's Tip

Remember that it may not be up to you to perform some inspections. If the sellers pay for the inspection, such as for pests, let them. That way the seller, inspector, and pest exterminator are liable for anything missed and not corrected. If you are buying directly from the seller, without financing, make sure an adequate pest inspection gets done.

There are other things you *can* inspect for, though. They are the red flags that tell you something's wrong. You can then require that a contractor repair problems before the sale is closed. Or you can negotiate the price based on after-sale repairs you may make. Just be sure your lender allows you to do this. Some want to make sure a licensed contractor has been engaged for any needed repairs. Make certain you account for the "reg flag" items in your original contract. Most sellers do not want to negotiate what isn't in the contract.

What can you inspect for? Here are some common red flags:

➤ Moisture problems: water where it shouldn't be, caused by inadequate drainage or even broken pipes.

➤ Mold and mildew.

➤ Cement damage: cracks or crumbling that indicates soil shifting, excessive water, or poor construction.

➤ Misalignment: walls that bow, windows and doors that stick, built-in cabinets that don't work smoothly, uneven flooring.

➤ Gaps: air leaks around windows and doors, loose windows and trim.

➤ Ground and slope: Look for water drainage paths, areas that can slide, and other potential ground problems.

➤ Heating and cooling systems: broken or inoperative controls, systems that repeatedly turn on and off, leaky ducting, clogged systems, fireplace damage and leaks.

Pitfall

Beware fresh paint, especially in a bathroom or kitchen, intended to cover up water marks or other damage. During your inspection, check shelves in the garage or storage for painting products intended to mask water marks and other telltale signs of hidden problems.

Even if you decide to hire a professional inspector, knowing what the inspector looks for can help you determine whether you are getting your money's worth from the inspector and from the seller.

Insider's Tip

Need to hire a professional residential inspector? Their largest trade association is the American Society of Home Inspectors (800-743-2744; www.ashi.org). You may find a local inspector by calling them or visiting their Web site. Or ask your lender. Make sure any inspector you hire is covered by errors and omissions insurance, just in case.

Lingo

Errors and omissions insurance is a liability insurance policy for professionals that covers mistakes and malpractice claims from their clients. Among the real estate pros who typically have E&O are brokers, agents, lenders, inspectors, and appraisers. As you hire professionals to do any real estate work for you, make sure they are covered by errors and omissions insurance.

Getting an Appraisal

As mentioned in chapter 12, you can hire an appraiser or you can do it yourself. Most lenders, however, will require a certified appraisal. Most lenders have a list of approved appraisers; if yours isn't on this list and cannot be added, they won't use him or her. Even so, it's a good idea to know how to verify the work of an appraiser.

Lingo

An *appraisal* is an estimate or opinion of property value. In addition to the sale and purchase of property, appraisals are made to determine property value at death or divorce for estate tax purposes as well as to determine property taxes.

Why would a professional appraiser *not* issue an accurate appraisal? Because the appraiser:

➤ Doesn't know the area or the neighborhood very well (but won't tell you so).

➤ Didn't do his or her homework, checking public records or even fully reading the sale documents.

➤ Hasn't kept up with recent market changes crucial to an accurate appraisal.

➤ Never even visited the property, relying instead on public records and maybe a drive-by.

➤ Does lots of business with or personally knows the seller, the lender, or others, and slants the appraisal to their benefit.

Insider's Tip

Need to hire a professional appraiser? The major trade association for real estate appraisers today is the Appraisal Institute (312-335-4100; www.appraisalinstitute.org).

Are these failures of service unethical? Certainly. Do they occur? Yes. Still, you can keep your appraiser honest by reading the appraisal, verifying facts, and discussing any discrepancies you find. Some may be honest mistakes. Others aren't.

Want to do your own appraisal or double-check a professional appraisal? Use the tools that pro appraisers use such as the Marshall & Swift *Residential Cost Handbook* (800-544-2678, www.marshallswift.com), localized to 825 locations. Other real estate appraisal books, such as the *National Building Cost Manual,* are published by Craftsman Book Company (800-829-8123, www.craftsman-book.com). You also can take a real estate appraisal class at many community colleges to help you develop the skills and the resources for making your own appraisal—and making it stick.

Knowing what you now know about appraisers and how they work, you can better hire an appraiser if needed. Depending on how you structure the purchase, you may wind up paying for the appraisal, or the seller may. In either case, know what you should be getting—and what to do about it if you don't.

Getting a Home Warranty

If you're concerned about things that may break down once you've bought the home, you can negotiate the price to include replacing or repairing things as needed. A thorough inspection will reveal most of the potential problems. Another option is to get a home warranty before you buy. The home warranty can take one of three forms:

➤ The seller agrees to replace any major appliance or pay for any major repair that occurs within the first 30, 90, or even 180 days after the home sale.

➤ The seller agrees to purchase home warranty insurance for you to cover replacement or repairs for a specified period. Read your home warranty policy thoroughly; if you want more coverage, it's not much more expensive to upgrade.

➤ You buy your own insurance or accept the risk of repairs or replacement in consideration for a reduction in the purchase price.

Any one of these methods works fine. Insurance is legalized gambling, so you want to make sure the risks are as low as possible, but you may find it easier and less expensive to self-insure rather than find an agent who will write a policy. You just don't want any surprises.

Pitfall

Some homeowner warranty policies are worth little to the buyer or the seller. The seller typically takes out the policy on behalf of the buyer through an insurance broker. The fine print may require a high deductible *and* that the service be done by a specific contractor, probably someone's brother-in-law. Or repeated calls to the insurer may go unanswered. That's why some buyers prefer to work directly with the seller on a warranty.

Summary

Doing your own homework makes sense. The more you know about a property you intend to purchase, the better you can understand what you're getting into. It also puts you in a better negotiating position because you can challenge false claims and verify potentially true ones. It gives you confidence as you make your offer to buy.

CHAPTER 16

Pulling the Money Together

*B*uying a home is an investment. To make the most of that investment, you must know all the costs (purchase, finance, closing)—*and* you must know how you're going to pay for it. You must pull the money together.

This chapter supplements what you learned about home financing in chapters 3 and 8. It covers closing costs because you are now your own agent and won't have someone to make sure they aren't excessive. It also gives you some tips on financing your home, including what you can do if your credit isn't perfect or you need a little more funding—called creative financing. You'll also learn how to protect yourself from unscrupulous lenders and sellers.

Funding the Purchase

Take a peek at chapter 8. Yes, you're buying property without an agent and chapter 8 is in the section about using an agent, but the same rules apply. The difference is that you don't have a professional adviser (the agent) to help you select the best lender, prequalify, and get the funding you need. You're on your own. Chapter 8 gives you an introduction to the topic of qualifying for a loan. This chapter will expand on it.

You want the lowest interest rates you can get. That's obvious. How can you get them? The same way you would buy a new car, a new refrigerator, or any other major purchase: You shop around. Use the annual percentage rate (APR) as the comparative fact. APR is defined by law as the effective (actual) rate of interest for a loan, per year. It includes *all* interest charges of the loan as well as points. It is the cost of your credit as a yearly rate. It's also called the *effective rate*. Your lender is required by law to give you a good-faith estimate within three days of opening your loan, spelling out exactly how much APR you will pay, lender fees, and how much you will be paying back.

Lingo

A *point* is prepaid interest. You reduce the long-term interest rate by prepaying some of the interest up front in what's called a *buy-down*. There are only certain times you should buy down your interest rate. The best time is when you plan to own the residence for at least five years. If not, you may not recoup the money you paid up front. Talk with a tax consultant for specifics.

Insider's Tip

Need to lower your interest rate? You can ask the seller to pay some points (prepaid interest) for you as part of the negotiations. Talk with your lender about how to do this and how much it will save you on the loan versus what you may have to trade off in the purchase price with the seller. You may also ask the seller to carry back a small second mortgage, making your first mortgage smaller—which in turn lowers your interest rate and helps you avoid mortgage insurance.

As you shop for mortgage financing, you'll learn that there are different rates for different borrowers. It's not discrimination, it's business. Lenders give better rates to borrowers who offer less risk of default. The greater the risk, the higher the rate.

So it's important to know what kind of borrower you are. Chapter 8 showed you how to get information on your credit history, called a credit report, as well as find out your FICO score. The FICO system calculates relative scores based on your payment history, how much credit you have, how long you've had that credit, how much new credit you've gotten recently, and what mix of credit you have (long-term, short-term, and so on). To get a mortgage through most lenders, you will need a FICO score of at least 680. That makes you a prime borrower. Less than 680 means you are considered subprime and will have to pay more interest, but chances are that you can still get a mortgage. If your score is below 550, you'll need some credit repair before any reputable lender (even a credit card company) will loan you money. *Note:* If you are a first-time buyer and don't have at least four pieces of credit, you will have trouble obtaining a loan. Your mortgage broker will suggest that you open a few credit card accounts, take out a car loan, and the like to create your "credit history" first.

Pitfall

Beware of interest rates that seem too good to be true. They probably are! Some lenders have escalation clauses that increase the interest rate over a short period of time. That's okay *if* it's clear and you know that's what you want. Many of them, however, hide the escalation in the fine print and, instead, promote the ridiculously low *initial* interest rate. Don't get scammed; read the fine print.

Where can you look for lenders? If you already have a mortgaged property, start by contacting the lender—if you want to give it future business. If your experience with the lender is bad, you may want to scratch it off the list. Also contact your bank, savings and loan, credit union, and others with whom you have a financial relationship. Why start with them? Because many have a slightly lower interest rate for what they call preferred customers, someone who already is doing business with them. If they don't, ask for one. In addition, if they are already in the transaction (paying off their mortgage, and so on), it will mean fewer new people in the transaction and less chance of errors or problems.

Pitfall

Beware so-called credit repair services. Many (not all) of them actually make consolidating loans at very high interest rates and, if you keep up payments, give you a good credit rating for the transaction. That doesn't *repair* your credit, it only adds a good mark to bad credit. Some are truly credit counseling services sponsored by the major credit reporting services. Why would they help you? Because your repaired credit benefits their customers, those who sell on credit. If you have credit problems, first call one of the credit reporting services (chapter 8) to find out what assistance you can get.

Also check larger daily newspapers in your area (or the new location where you plan to buy) for current mortgage rates. Many papers have a small graphic table, at least in the Sunday edition, that compares various mortgage lenders' rates for fifteen- and thirty-year fixed and adjustable mortgages. Be careful. Some of these comparative tables are actually advertisements or are sponsored by one or more lenders, meaning you may not get all the facts.

Insider's Tip

Want to know what current mortgage rates are? You can check on the Internet at mortgagerates.com, bankrate.com, and on the Federal Trade Commission's Web site at ftc.gov. You also can calculate payment differences for various mortgage interest rates at mortgage-calc.com.

Should you get your next mortgage lender off the television or the Internet? Some lenders seem to be spending lots of money to lure us to finance or refinance through them. Is it a pitfall? Most are legitimate, using television to promote their services to the widest audience. As with all other mortgage sources, however, make sure you know their *effective rate* or APR and check the fine print for hidden closing costs and escalation clauses. Some verbally say "No fees" but add them in anyway! Carefully read your loan papers.

Preparing Other Assets

Money you borrow isn't the only asset you may have to help you buy the house or apartment you want. You may have a home to sell, cars or trucks that you no longer need, stocks or bonds to sell, business assets, or other things you can liquidate to make your home purchase. Making a major purchase like a house or apartment is a good time to turn little-used assets into more money for your home.

The biggest trick is buying a new home subject to the sale of your current home. Many sellers don't want to sell based on the *possible* sale of your home. They may require that your home be in escrow or closing—or at least be offered at a value price in a fast-moving marketplace. If you are making an offer to buy subject to your sale, make sure you can make the best case for why sellers should accept this contingency. Remember, the sellers are taking their home off the market. You'll need to give them a good reason to do so. Smart sellers will include a clause that releases them from your offer within one to three days if they get a noncontingency offer. Be a smart buyer and either stay away from such contingencies or negotiate a longer release with the seller.

As you fill out the loan application, review each of the assets and liabilities that you list to determine if there are any you can sell or clear. Doing so will put you in a better bargaining position with the lender and make purchasing your next home easier.

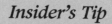

Insider's Tip

Some lenders can help you through the transition when you may have two homes. If your credit rating is good, you have lots of equity in your current home, and the market in which you are selling is strong, you can ask your current lender for a *bridge loan*. This is a loan on your new home based on your current home's equity and your credit rating. Your current home doesn't have to sell first. The lender just wants to make sure that you can afford to pay two mortgages for a while. It's not for everyone, but it can allow you to buy your next home without a contingency for selling your existing home.

Creative Financing

Many of us stretch our income to the limit, hopefully not exceeding it! That means we may not have the money needed for a down payment or to make monthly payments for the first year or two. Fortunately, there are creative options.

When looking for down payment money, consider:

➤ Loans that require a smaller down payment.

➤ Borrowing against the cash value of your life insurance.

➤ Selling or refinancing a car, boat, or other vehicles.

➤ Selling or refinancing vacation property, vacant land, or other real estate.

➤ Gifts or loans from relatives or friends.

➤ Income tax refunds or loans against filed refunds.

➤ Credit line or letter of credit from a bank.

➤ Sweat equity—doing some of the needed repairs in exchange for a lowered down payment.

➤ Longer close of escrow (two to three months) to give you time to gather cash for the down payment.

➤ If you have a home business, get a Small Business Administration (SBA) loan first.

➤ The seller contributes to your down payment (or prepays interest points).

➤ The seller lends you a small second mortgage on the house.

➤ The seller acts as lender and carries the first mortgage so you avoid those lender fees.

Insider's Tip

Don't expect the seller to give you the down payment in exchange for a higher selling price. This type of sale puts all the risk on the seller, and few are willing to do it—unless there are other reasons why the seller *must* unload the property. Some sellers will assist you with the down payment if a large one is required, but will ask for something in return.

➤ The seller offers alternative financing for tax advantages regarding basis.

Lingo

Basis is the value of a property for taxation purposes. Due to depreciation, the seller may be required to pay additional taxes on any price over the property's basis valuation. It gets complicated and requires a tax attorney. Still, some sellers may offer a property at a lower price (near their basis) and ask for other terms in order to avoid taxation. If you get involved in such a transaction, make sure you get an attorney or tax adviser involved, too.

There are many other ways of creating financing for your next house or apartment. The rules are: Keep your mind open to new ideas, investigate each idea to make sure you're not missing something, and ask for or hire advice to help you make the best decision.

Estimating Closing Costs

Another important part of putting the money together for your house is making sure that you have enough cash to cover closing costs. What are closing costs? They are the various fees and expenses the buyer and seller pay when the transaction is closed and title is transferred. They are also known as transaction costs. Typical closing costs include:

➤ Real estate commissions (seller).

➤ Lender points and fees (buyer).

➤ Title insurance premium (buyer or seller).

➤ Document preparation and recording fees (seller).

➤ Pest inspection fees (seller).

➤ Home inspection fees (buyer or seller).

➤ Appraisal fees (buyer).

➤ Attorney fees (seller or buyer).

➤ Escrow and notary fees (seller and buyer).

➤ Prorated taxes (buyer).

➤ One year's homeowner insurance (buyer).

➤ Prepaid interest (buyer).

➤ Escrow or impound account reserves and costs (buyer).

Who pays each of the fees is negotiable. The seller may pay some or all of the buyer fees or vice versa in exchange for other concessions. For example, the seller may require a full-price offer but will pay some or all of the buyer closing costs. Or the buyer may offer to buy at a reduced price but will pay some or all of the seller closing costs. Negotiating closing costs is a good option when putting together a deal that works for both the buyer and seller. Sellers might also credit back money for repairs that need to be done that they don't want to do before close of escrow.

Pitfall

Closings typically involve numerous delivery and miscellaneous fees, many of them unnecessary. An overnight delivery fee of $25 or $50, for example, is only required with an expedited closing. Most closings can run smoothly with U.S. Postal Service delivery at a tenth the price. You can't watch every charge, but you can make sure that the closing officer knows you're watching the bill and will reject any unnecessary expenses at closing.

I'll give more information on closing or settlement costs in chapter 18, "Closing on Your Castle."

Estimating Time

How long will closing take? How long do you *want* it to take? If you're trying to get your existing home sold or need more time to sell assets and save for a down payment, you can stretch the closing date out as long as the seller is willing to. It, too, is negotiable. If you have the cash you need and there are few contingencies, however, you can close a home in less than ten days. More typical is fourteen to thirty days from the time the RPA or sales contract is signed by all parties.

So the closing time is really dependent on the contingencies of your offer to buy. Your lender can estimate how long it will take to process papers and get funding, inspectors can estimate how long it will take to inspect and report on the property, and an appraiser can estimate appraisal reporting time. Because *you* are the transaction manager, not an agent, you will need to get these estimates and crack the whip to keep everyone working toward the common goal.

Insider's Tip

When estimating time to close on a property, remember to ask participants whether it is consecutive to or concurrent with other tasks. For example, the appraiser may need only one week, but it must be after the lender has issued preliminary loan approval. Make a schedule that includes all contingencies and how long it will take to get them removed or signed off.

Summary

For most home buyers, pulling the money together is critical to buying the house or apartment they want. They must fund the purchase through financing or selling off other assets, or using creative financing. To make sure they have enough money to close, they must estimate closing costs and time. Only then are they ready to make an offer—and make it stick.

CHAPTER 17

Making an Offer and Making It Stick

*F*or many people, making the offer to the seller is where their knees go soft. They can handle the research and even the financing, but when it comes to negotiating they reconsider hiring an agent to do the "dirty work."

Actually, with a little training and a few insider tips you can do as well as an agent—and save thousands of dollars. In fact, you may even be able to do better than many agents because you care more about the outcome. It's not just a commission check, it's your home!

Having been on both sides of the table many times as agent, buyer, and seller, I can offer some advice that will put your mind at ease and make you wonder why you ever thought making an offer was difficult. You can do this, too.

Setting the Price and Terms

How much should you offer the seller for the property? As discussed in earlier chapters, everything is negotiable, depending on what the seller's needs are. So the first step to answering this question is understanding the seller.

As you have researched this property, you've probably learned much about the sellers, why they *say* they are selling, the probable reasons why they *are* selling, an estimate of the number of other buyers who may be interested in the property, and even how much flexibility there may be in the asking price or terms. Remember, you want facts rather than opinions because you'll use these facts to support your offer when you present it.

Also put yourself in the sellers' shoes for a moment. If you've talked with the sellers at length, you may know which of them is more interested in selling and why. You need to understand their motivations because you are going to present the offer in a nonconfrontational way (I'll show you how), and knowing how to do it means understanding what the sellers are thinking.

Okay. Let's get to putting some numbers on scratch paper. Write down the asking price as well as amounts 5 and 10 percent below the asking price. Much depends on whether the local real estate marketplace is hot or cold as well as how long the property has been offered for sale, but these three figures give you the price range in a *typical* (warm) marketplace. Only newly offered properties and those offered in hot marketplaces will expect the full asking price. Most properties that have been on the market more than thirty days will consider offers about 5 percent lower than the asking price. If the property is on longer, they may accept a 10 percent or even greater reduction.

Having said that, let me add that you may not want to lower the asking price as much as you can. You may be better off paying near the asking price and requesting other term concessions such as short or long closing, seller paying some of your closing costs or taking a second mortgage, leaving major appliances, or other compromises. Remember that a $10,000 increase in a 5 percent, thirty-year mortgage adds only $53.70 to the monthly payment. Is there some other concession you need more than fifty-four bucks a month?

Insider's Tip

If you are offering a price lower than the asking price, defend your offer with a market analysis or an appraisal. A $300 appraisal expense may save you many thousands of dollars on an over-priced home. You may have to write your offer subject to an appraisal because the seller won't allow an appraiser access until the home is in escrow.

Writing the Offer

You previously learned that *all* terms of a real estate transaction must be in writing. Real estate agents use a preprinted, multiple-copy form called the Residential Purchase Agreement (RPA). You will use a standardized form called a Purchase Agreement or Land Purchase Agreement. You can buy these through local stationery stores or online. Just make sure you get ones that don't include clauses for agents and commissions.

Standard purchase agreements typically include the same components no matter what state they are written in. Typical paragraphs are:

➤ Date of offer.

➤ Offer (legal description, price offered).

➤ Contingencies or conditions.

➤ Financing or other sources of funds.

➤ Date and time of the closing and of occupancy.

➤ Allocation of costs (who pays for what).

➤ Disclosures of the property's condition.

➤ Time frames for inspections and repairs, along with who pays for what.

➤ Title warranties.

➤ Sale of buyer's property (if required).

➤ Dispute resolution.

➤ Other conditions.

➤ Joint escrow instructions.

➤ Places for seller and buyer to sign and date.

➤ The amount of time that the seller has to respond.

Some standardized forms include instructions or a telephone help line for questions. They cannot give you legal or real estate advice, but they may be able to help you complete the form.

Insider's Tip

Make sure that any standardized forms you purchase and use are legal in the state in which the property is located. Real estate laws vary among states—sometimes slightly, sometimes significantly. A lender or an escrow service won't accept a countersigned purchase agreement that doesn't conform to state laws.

Another option is to hire an attorney to draw up the purchase agreement. This is obviously an expense for you, but it will be minimal compared to the potential loss if there is a legal dispute. In addition, most sellers would prefer to see an offer drawn up by a trusted local attorney than one that was purchased at a stationery store.

Note that some condominium, cooperative apartment, and townhouse sellers have their own preprinted form for writing the offer and may require that you use this, or use an attorney. Some sellers of subdivisions and all foreclosure companies require that their own forms be completed.

Insider's Tip

How long should you give the seller to accept the offer you've written? Long enough for careful consideration but short enough to keep other buyers from presenting their offer before yours is accepted. Also, if the seller is in a distant location or there are sellers in various locations, you need to allow enough time for transit of the agreement copies. An in-town deal may allow two to four days for acceptance, depending on the seller's needs and the speed of the marketplace.

Presenting the Offer

Congratulations—you're ready to present your offer to purchase the house or apartment you want!

Your first step in presenting this offer is contacting the seller and asking for an appointment. You want to make sure that all owners are in attendance and that there will be few distractions. Often the offer is presented at the seller's home, with all sellers and all buyers present. If there are young children, you may have to wait until they are in bed.

How you actually present the offer depends on what's in it. Professional agents typically review all the positives in detail, then note any negatives. Positives are any of the seller's terms that the buyer accepts without change—perhaps the price, closing date, or other conditions. If you don't require financing and can pay cash for the property, say so up front. That's certainly a plus for most sellers, because financing can delay a sale. If you have mortgage preapproval, note that as well.

Insider's Tip

Your offer to purchase should include a good-faith down payment on the transaction, called the *earnest money*. The larger the amount, the more you will impress the seller that you are in earnest. How much earnest money is enough? Typically 1 to 2 percent of the purchase price is acceptable, though more may be needed to impress a seller asked to accept some contingencies. Write the check (payable to an escrow service or title company) and include it in your presentation.

The negatives may be some conditions that the seller will reluctantly accept, or they may be deal-breakers. The more negative you think the response will be, the more you will need to prepare reasons the condition isn't as bad as it seems. For example:

➤ *We require ninety days to close on the property but can give you assurances of loan approval after just thirty days.*

➤ *We must sell our current home, but it is currently on the market and we have an offer coming in the next five days.*

➤ *If we can't get the financing we want within sixty days, my uncle says he will co-sign for us.*

➤ *We have an inspector standing by to check the property and can remove the contingency within two weeks.*

➤ *Yes, we are offering $20,000 less than your asking price, but we can close on the property within two weeks so you can move on to your new job.*

➤ *The price we are offering is lower than your asking price, so we will hire an appraiser and will abide by the valuation.*

You get the idea. Start by getting agreement on the positive aspects of your offer and work toward those you believe will be less acceptable to the seller. You may be pleasantly surprised to find that, with clear description and responsive discussion, all of the terms are acceptable and you will soon own your new home.

Insider's Tip

Still not sure you want to present the offer to the sellers yourself? Hire a real estate attorney to do so. Not only will this impress most sellers, but the attorney can play bad cop: "The buyers may not be able to accept your changes, so let's discuss them." Your attorney can negotiate for you, possibly getting you a better deal that will more than cover her or his fee. Another option at this point is to hire a real estate agent to handle the transaction for you at a dramatically reduced fee. It's legal!

Handling Counteroffers

But what if not all your terms are acceptable to the seller? Even after you have found agreement over most of the offer's points, there may still be a few conditions that the seller won't accept. What can you do?

The seller can make you a counteroffer, often by adding to or changing the purchase agreement you've written. If you expect a counteroffer, it's wise to bring along a standard counteroffer addendum form for changes. It will say something like "We, the sellers, accept all the terms of the buyer's purchase agreement with the following changes . . ."

Insider's Tip

Remind the sellers that if they sign your purchase agreement without changes, the deal is made. If they make a single change to it, however, the deal is incomplete until you, the buyer, agree to the counteroffers. If you don't, the seller cannot go back to the original deal and accept it without your approval.

Make sure that the final purchase agreement refers to any specific counteroffers made. Unless they are referenced in the agreement, they are not legally part of it. In addition, the seller and buyer must sign and date the purchase agreement and any addendums, including a counteroffer. Remember that time is of the essence. If you exceed your time limit, the other party can claim "Null and void" and accept another offer.

Insider's Tip

Remember that the best deals are those where both the buyer and the seller get what they want. This means there is less of a chance of a lawsuit. As you negotiate, remind the seller that you both want the same thing: a successful transaction under terms that you both can live with.

Escrowing the Sale

Seller and buyer have signed the purchase agreement and any addendums. Now what? You must agree on who will escrow the transaction. If you are using a lender, ask the seller to use it as the escrow service or to recommend one. The advantage to seller and buyer is that the escrow cost (which is typically shared) will probably be lower than if you used a complete escrow service.

Insider's Tip

Counteroffers and counter-counteroffers can make the transaction difficult for an escrow officer to follow. Rather than counter a counteroffer, it's best to write a new purchase agreement with the agreed-upon terms and get it signed by all sellers and buyers. An error in escrow instructions can cost time in closing—or it can cost money if nobody catches it. Time is of the essence.

All you need to start the closing escrow is a copy of the purchase agreement and addendums, along with any agreed-upon earnest money. It's best to deliver the papers and money to escrow on the first business day after the seller and buyer have signed the agreement. The escrow officer will make sure the following points are clear on the purchase agreement:

➤ The agreed-upon close-of-escrow date.

➤ The buyer's name, address, and phone number for contacting during escrow and for mailing the title report and possibly the closing papers.

➤ The seller's name, address, and phone number for contacting during escrow.

➤ The property address, parcel number, tax ID number, legal description, or other identifiers.

➤ The type of dwelling (single-family residence, condominium, cooperative apartment, town house, or other type).

➤ The name and address of any homeowner association for which there are dues payable.

➤ Whether the property is occupied and, if so, by whom.

➤ The sale price, terms, earnest money deposit, contingencies, and deadlines.

➤ The name, contact information, and loan number for any existing mortgage(s) on the property.

➤ The name and contact information for the buyer's lender, if any.

➤ The agreed-upon inspections and who pays for them.

➤ The home insurance agent.

➤ Additional instructions (which must be in writing and countersigned!).

The escrow service or officer will set up an escrow account into which the earnest money, lender's money, and any cash you're supplying will be deposited. Inspection, title, escrow, and other costs will be deducted from the account unless instructions say otherwise. At closing, there will be a full accounting of all receipts and disbursements from the account—it's the law. The escrow will give the buyers title and the sellers their proceeds from the sale, and will pay any other lien holders (such as the seller's mortgagor). That's called closing, and it's covered in greater detail in the next and final chapter.

> ## Insider's Tip
>
> Even though you aren't using a real estate agent, review part 2 of this book for tips on how professional agents make an offer to the seller that they believe will get them a commission check.

Summary

Don't be intimidated by the thought of making a formal offer to the seller. The seller wants a successful transaction as much as you do! Instead, set the price and terms you believe will be acceptable, write the offer using standard forms or an attorney, present the offer yourself or through an attorney, and put the agreement into escrow. In no time, you'll be living in your new house or apartment!

CHAPTER 18

Closing on Your Castle

*T*his is the day you've been working for. After signing perfunctory paperwork, you'll get the keys to your new-to-you home and can move in.

But not so fast! That pile of papers is important and needs your undivided attention. Within it are unintentional errors and intentional sneak-bys that can cost you money. So don't stop being diligent. Don't depend on the so-called experts to make closing day go well. It's *your* money!

Planning for a Smooth Closing

Closing is the event when buyer and seller sign papers and trade assets to officially transfer title of a specific property. Leading up to all this are smaller events intended to satisfy conditions of the residential purchase agreement (RPA), including financing, inspections, and other contingencies. So the best way to plan for a smooth closing is to make sure each of the RPA's conditions is met *and* approved in writing.

As soon as your offer to purchase has been approved by the seller, you can start mapping the process needed to take you to closing. Use your Buyer's Notebook to list the conditions of the sale, then the steps you must take to satisfy each one. For example, you might list the condition "Subject to Financing" and, beneath it:

➤ Complete a Uniform Residential Loan Application (URLA).

➤ Analyze and select the three best mortgage lenders for this property.

➤ Meet with each lender to review my URLA and find out exactly what terms the lender can offer *before* submitting my application to the one with the best terms.

➤ Once the loan app is approved, get it *in writing* and get a copy to the escrow service so it knows that the financing condition has been met.

Once you've developed a plan for each condition, you have a map of the things that need to be done before the property can go to closing. Remember to also include any deadlines required by the purchase agreement. If you need to have financing within fifteen days, this becomes a higher priority than any conditions with thirty-day time lines.

The next step in mapping the journey to closing is listing all tasks by priority. For example:

1. Complete the URLA.

2. Hire a building inspector and set an appointment with the seller for the inspection.

3. Contact the moving company about setting a tentative date to pack and move.

As you can see, the map is simply a list of all specific tasks ranked by importance and time frame. You don't want to get all the way to the closing date before you realize that you forgot to hire an inspector or call the mover. A buyer's agent is paid to help you plan and manage these details; you are saving money by doing these things yourself.

Early Occupancy and Other Challenges

Some contingencies or conditions are easier to satisfy than others. If you are prequalified for the loan (chapters 3, 8, and 16), you may be able to sign off on the financing contingency in just a few days. Other conditions, however, may require more time or work. Early occupancy is often one of them.

Insider's Tip

A little short on funds? You can typically lower closing costs by setting a closing date later in the month (due to prorations). This also may mean, however, that your first payment is due sooner. Ask your escrow officer about your options. If appropriate, ask about a discount on escrow fees for first-time home buyers! Many offer a 10 to 25 percent discount.

Most closings don't allow the buyers to occupy the property until they legally own it. In some transactions, though, the buyer has requested and received an early-occupancy clause in the purchase agreement. It may be because the seller is willing to move out early based on the buyer's prequalified financing or because the seller has already moved out and the property is vacant. In any case, the buyer is allowed to move into the subject property *as a renter*. Thus, there needs to be a separate rental agreement between the seller and buyer. Make sure that the terms of the rental are clearly spelled out in this separate agreement. Who pays for repairs once the buyer moves in is very important! Also make sure that the lender and the escrow service are aware of this agreement.

Insider's Tip

Make sure that *all* contingencies are removed or signed off *in writing*. Your escrow service can tell you how. You don't want to delay closing because you forgot to sign off on a condition when it was removed.

On the other side of the coin, you, the buyer, may prefer to take occupancy sometime *after* title is transferred. This may be because the seller found and closed on a home quickly, but can't get out of a current home or location as fast. In this case, you may prefer to close on the home but allow the seller to live there for a while *as a renter*.

Early-occupancy rental agreements have gotten a bad name because they haven't always been treated as separate rental agreements between the seller and buyer. The more informal they are, the greater the chances that problems will delay closing. What can go wrong?

> ➤ The buyer (that's you!) can get cold feet and decide to cancel the sale by not fulfilling conditions of the purchase agreement.

> ➤ The buyer may notice lots of items in need of repair that were overlooked during the inspections.

> ➤ The seller can charge excessively for occupancy, then slow the closing process to earn more rent.

If you are concerned about drawing up a rental agreement that protects you, hire a real estate attorney to do the job rather than relying on a standard rental agreement form. Note that some real estate purchase agreement forms include a section for terms of occupancy other than on the date that title is transferred. Look for this type of form if you expect to have issues of early or late occupancy in the transaction. A well-written early-occupancy agreement can make moving easier for the buyer and/or seller while satisfying the requirements of a timely and efficient closing. That's your goal!

Preclosing Review

Important events such as weddings, live performances, and property transfers benefit from having a rehearsal to minimize problems that can diminish the actual event. I strongly recommend that you require and take advantage of a preclosing review with the lender, escrow service, or whoever else is handling the closing. Doing so can catch any errors and make closing smoother.

Don't forget to also do a walk-through inspection of the property at least five days before close of escrow. Standard contracts note that the property (inside and out) should be in the same condition at this point as when you made the offer. Check for cared-for landscaping, clean walls, carpets, floors, window coverings, screens, and any attached items not excluded in your offer. Rubbish, tools, old boats, wood, and the like should be removed.

Why is this review important? Because the escrow service is paid to bring everything to a culmination on a particular date. Loan payments, taxes, and payoffs are all prorated to the specific date when the escrow service believes that all contingencies will be satisfied and the transfer of assets between seller and buyer can happen.

So make sure that the escrow service you use in this transaction knows that you require a preclosing review. Most will set it up within forty-eight hours of the scheduled closing. The seller may ask for a preclosing review as well, and you can combine the events.

Insider's Tip

Asking for a preclosing review puts escrow services on notice that you want to verify each charge. Some will welcome this, while others will do so reluctantly. In any case, you are telling the service that you are a careful consumer who wants to know where every dollar goes. It's *your* money.

What should you be looking for during a preclosing review? Mostly potential errors in disbursements among the seller, buyer, and lenders. They can be math errors, but more often they involve mistakes over who pays for what or "standard fees" that are charged without the service being performed.

Closing, as you've learned, is also called the settlement. Closing costs are settlement costs. Most closing transactions follow the federal Department of Housing and Urban Development (HUD) guidelines for settlement costs. Settlement statements include a description of the property and the loan as well as a summary of the transaction for the borrower and one for the seller. The summary of the borrower's transaction will include:

➤ The gross amount due *from* the buyer.

➤ Adjustments for items paid *or* unpaid by the seller in advance, including taxes and assessments.

➤ The amounts paid by or for the borrower, including the earnest money deposit and the principal amount of new loans.

➤ The cash to be paid by or to the borrower at settlement (closing); this must be a cashier's check, or the transaction may have to wait until a personal check clears.

The seller will have a transaction summary as well, including:

➤ The gross amount due *to* the seller.

➤ Adjustments for items paid *or* unpaid by the seller in advance, including taxes and assessments.

➤ Reductions in the amount due to the seller, including settlement charges to the seller, as well as existing loans and their payoffs.

➤ The cash to be paid by the seller at settlement (closing).

Why are these components nearly identical? Because the bottom lines for both the seller and the buyer *must be equal*. What's put into the transaction must be equal in value to what is taken out. It's the escrow service's job to make sure the two are equal. The settlement summary includes a list of who paid how much for:

➤ Sales or broker's commissions (if any).

➤ Loan and credit report fees.

➤ Appraisal and inspection fees.

➤ Mortgage broker and other service fees.

➤ Prorated taxes and insurance.

➤ Reserve deposits: hazard and mortgage insurance, taxes, and assessments.

➤ Transfer charges, recording fees, and sales taxes.

➤ Other charges.

Insider's Tip

Not all settlement fees are necessarily included in the settlement summary. Credit reports and appraisals may be paid outside of closing or escrow, depending on what the seller and buyer agree upon. If so, they may be listed on the settlement as *paid outside of closing* or POC.

You can see why it's best to check over each of these charges and credits *before* the day when you must sign for them. On closing day, any corrections or changes may delay the transaction!

As you review the settlement statement, ask the escrow officer or clerk any "dumb" questions you wish. There is less pressure during a preclosing review than at the closing event, and the representative will typically have more time to explain each charge. Also, bring your calculator or ask the clerk to recalculate all costs as you review them.

Signing Your Life Away

If you've had a preclosing review of the settlement documents, the actual signing of those (corrected) documents will be faster and less stressful. You can simply verify that the requested changes were made and sign them. You and any other buyers in the transaction can still ask questions, however, and even get changes made.

Insider's Tip

What happens if you or the sellers find a problem with the closing papers that must be resolved before you will sign? With minor changes or errors, you may be able to simply write in the corrected data and initial it. If the sellers have already signed off without seeing the error, or if the error affects other parts of the papers, the escrow service may prefer to recalculate and redraw the papers for new signatures. This can delay signing and closing by anywhere from a few hours to a few days, depending on the problem. If it involves a serious misunderstanding between seller and buyer based on ambiguous instructions in the purchase agreement, a third party such as an attorney may need to step in before closing papers can be fully signed. Taking care of situations *before* they become problems is your best option.

The escrow service will tell you if you need to bring a check to closing, what kind it should be (cashier's or certified), and for how much. If it's a personal check, you'll probably need to wait until it clears the banks (up to ten days) before the sale can close.

Also, make sure that *all* owners of the property are available for the signing. If some are in another location, the escrow officer will need to send papers to them by courier, possibly delaying the closing.

In most transactions—depending on state laws and local customs—the seller and the buyer don't sit down at the table and sign at the same time. Many escrow services hold a seller's signing and a buyer's signing. If one or more parties to the transaction are out of the area, there may be two or more signings, as needed, to get everyone in agreement *in writing*. The escrow service will also notarize your signature, so don't forget your personal identification!

Recording and Disbursement

The transaction isn't done until the papers are delivered to the appropriate courthouse and accepted by the clerk for recording. At this point, the property transfer becomes public record, the money is dispersed by the escrow service, and you own a home.

After the transaction is completed, it is reviewed by the escrow service and all lenders involved. If the date of closing is different from the estimated date of closing, you or the seller may receive small checks in the mail to cover any excess payments made by one party or the other. Remember that the prorations and some fees are based on the date of recording, with some room for changes.

Your celebration of ownership is triggered by the recorder reporting that the transfer documents have been duly received and are part of the public record. You'll probably hear about this from the escrow service or the lender. In fact, you can request that one of them call you once the documents are officially recorded.

Moving In

Depending on the occupancy terms of your purchase agreement, you may be packed and ready to move in once the sale is recorded. As a courtesy, contact the sellers to verify when they will be out of the property so you can coordinate moving in. Also verify that the property will be cleaned of any debris.

Insider's Tip

Take an hour or two before you move the first box in to look over your new property, inspecting it for condition, personal property purchased with the house or apartment, and debris left behind. Take photos of any discrepancies. Make sure you are getting what you paid for.

If you haven't done so already, this is a good time to change the electricity, phone, gas, cable, and so on, into your name.

You're going to be anxious to sleep in your new home immediately. Still, remember that you will have many nights there; it's smarter to take your time and make the right move. Your Buyer's Notebook probably contains moving lists as well, including who gets what room, where major furniture and appliances will go, and who is going to make the physical move (you, friends, a mover). Just as in buying a house, following a plan to move in makes the job smoother.

Moving On

A final congratulations! Welcome to your new home. Now you can move on with the other things in your life that make it enjoyable. Keep in mind that moving is not just physical, it's emotional—especially for younger people. Those who haven't moved many times may not understand that life goes on. They may be feeling that life has stopped. Fears of additional losses can injure them. Be conscious of this and consider how you can make purchasing and living in your new home *more* secure for each of the individuals who made this trip with you.

May the Source of all good things give you joy to share with others.

Summary

Whew! You've finally reached your goal of buying a house, condo, co-op, or town house that will improve your life. You just made it through the most challenging part, dealing with the details of closing. You're moved in! And you did it by relying on trustworthy experts as well as making yourself an expert in buying a home or apartment.

Appendix A
Real Estate Glossary

Addendum

an attachment to a contract that becomes part of the contract.

Adjustable rate mortgage (ARM)

a mortgage loan that allows the interest rate to be changed at specific intervals over the term of the loan.

Agent

a state-licensed real estate broker *or* salesperson who performs services on behalf of the seller or buyer of real property.

Amortization

a gradual paying off of a debt by periodic installments.

Annual percentage rate (APR)

the effective (actual) rate of interest for a loan, per year, including *all* interest charges of the loan as well as points, or prepaid interest.

Appraisal

an estimate or opinion of property value.

Basis

the value of a property for taxation purposes, after depreciation.

Broker

a state-licensed real estate agent who, for a fee, acts on behalf of property sellers or buyers.

Buydown

prepaying interest (see *point*) at closing to reduce the long-term interest rate.

Buyer's agent

an agent hired by a buyer to negotiate with the seller or the seller's agent to purchase specific property.

Buyer's market	when buyers have a wide choice of properties because of local economic downturns or other factors.
Close (verb)	to transfer the ownership of a specific property.
Closing (noun)	the event when sellers and buyers sign final papers effecting the ownership transfer.
Condominium or **condo**	real property with individually owned units and jointly owned common property such as hallways, parking, and lawns.
Co-op	ownership in a corporation that collectively owns and shares property rights to a group of cooperative apartments.
Easement	the right, interest, or privilege that one party has in the land of another.
Equity	the value of a property above any liens against it.
Errors and omissions insurance	a liability insurance policy for professionals covering mistakes and malpractice claims from their clients.
Escrow	an agreement between two or more parties to allow a disinterested third party to manage a transaction following agreed-upon instructions.
Escrow account	a separate account into which funds are deposited and withdrawn for a specific real estate transaction.
Fee absolute	the owner of the real property has absolute ownership, can sell or otherwise dispose of the property during his or her lifetime, and can will the rights of ownership to another upon the owner's demise.
Fee simple	same as *fee absolute*.

First mortgage   a mortgage that has priority as a lien over all other mortgages.

Foreclosure   the termination of a mortgagee's right of redemption.

Interest rate   the cost of the use of money, expressed as a percentage.

Lien   a claim against the title of a property. A mortgage is a general lien. Subcontractors can file a mechanic's lien.

Life estate   an interest in real property that expires on the death of an owner or another specified person.

Loan-to-value (LTV) ratio   the ratio of the mortgage to the purchase price.

Manufactured home   a home constructed in a factory and moved to the building site by truck. In some states, manufactured or mobile homes are considered personal property unless attached to a permanent foundation.

Mortgage   a legal document that creates a lien against real estate as security toward payment of a specified debt.

Multiple listing service (MLS)   an association of real estate brokers who agree to share listings with each other.

Personal property   everything not attached to the land.

Point   prepaid interest.

Private mortgage insurance (PMI)   an insurance policy required by many lenders when the loan-to-value ratio is above 80 percent.

Property   the rights one individual has in land or goods to the exclusion of all others.

Real estate   the land and everything attached to it.

Real estate associate	a salesperson who works as an employee for a broker.
Real property	the right to use real estate.
Realtor	a licensed real estate agent who also is a member of the National Association of Realtors (NAR).
Second mortgage	a lien against the property that is second or subordinate to the rights of the first mortgage lien.
Seller's market	when there is a greater demand for housing than the supply offers, giving sellers a perceived advantage in pricing and selling their property.
Single-family residence (SFR)	a residential structure designed for use by one living group, either detached from or attached to (see *town house*) other residences.
Square foot	an area one foot wide by one foot deep.
Subagent	a real estate agent who works with the seller's agent to sell a home, typically through a multiple listing service.
Tenancy	the right of possession of real estate, including the right of ownership and occupancy, as defined by state laws.
Title	the evidence of ownership of a specific parcel of real estate.
Title insurance	an insurance policy protecting the buyer from loss due to defects in the title such as outstanding liens or uncleared ownership.
Title report	a summary of the current condition of the title of a specific parcel.

Town house a residence of two or more stories that shares common walls with other town houses.

Trust account see *escrow account.*

Valuation the estimated worth or price, or the act of estimating value.

Additional and more extensive definitions of real estate terms are included in the *Dictionary of Real Estate Terms,* fifth edition (Hauppauge, NY: Barron's Educational Series, Inc., 2000), available at larger bookstores or online at www.mulliganbooks.com.

Appendix B
Real Estate Resources

Real Estate Trade Associations

American Homeowners
Foundation
6776 Little Falls Road
Arlington, VA 22213-1213
Phone: 703-536-7776
Fax: 703-536-7776

American Institute of Architects
1735 New York Avenue, NW
Washington, DC 20006
Web site: www.aiaonline.com

American Land Title Association
1828 L Street, NW, Suite 705
Washington, DC 20036
Web site: www.alta.org

American Planning Association
122 South Michigan Avenue,
Suite 1600
Chicago, IL 60603
Phone: 312-431-9100
Fax: 312-431-9985
Web site: www.planning.org

American Real Estate & Urban
Economics Association
Indiana University, Kelley School of
Business
1309 East 10th Street, Suite 738

Bloomington, IN 47405
Web site: www.areuea.org

American Real Estate Society
Cleveland State University
Department of Finance—BU327E
Cleveland, OH 44114
Web site: www.aresnet.org

American Resort Development
Association
200 East Robinson Street, Suite 1170
Orlando, FL 32801
Phone: 407-245-7601
Fax: 407-872-0771
Web site: www.arda.org

American Society of Appraisers
555 Herndon Parkway, Suite 125
Herndon, VA 20170
Web site: www.appraisers.org

American Society of Farm Managers
& Rural Appraisers
950 South Cherry Street, Suite 508
Denver, CO 80222
Web site:
www.agri-association.org/asfmra

American Society of Home
Inspectors, Inc.
932 Lee Street, Suite 101
Des Plaines, IL 60016

Phone: 800-743-ASHI
Fax: 847-759-1620
Web site: www.ashi.org

Appraisal Foundation
1029 Vermont Avenue, NW,
Suite 900
Washington, DC 20005
Phone: 202-347-7722
Fax: 202-347-7727
Web site: www.
appraisalfoundation.org

Appraisal Institute
875 North Michigan Avenue,
Suite 2400
Chicago, IL 60611
Phone: 312-335-4100
Web site:
www.appraisalinstitute.org

Association of Appraiser Regulatory
Officials
c/o Kentucky Real Estate Appraisers
Board
1025 Capitol Center Drive, Suite 100
Frankfort, KY 40601
Phone: 502-573-0091
Fax: 502-573-0093

Building Owners & Managers
Association International
1201 New York Avenue, NW, Suite 300
Washington, DC 20005
Phone: 202-408-2662
Web site: www.boma.org

Commercial Investment Real Estate
Institute
430 North Michigan Avenue,
Suite 800
Chicago, IL 60611
Phone: 313-321-4460
Web site: www.ccim.com

Community Association Research
Foundation
1630 Duke Street
Alexandria, VA 22314
Phone: 703-548-8600
Fax: 703-684-1581

Community Associations Institute
225 Reinekers Lane, Suite 300
Alexandria, VA 22314
Phone: 703-548-8600
Fax: 703-684-1581
Web site: www.caionline.org

Consumer Federation of America
1424 16th Street, NW, Suite 604
Washington, DC 20036
Phone: 202-387-6121
Web site: www.consumerfed.org

Council of Real Estate Brokerage
Managers
430 North Michigan Avenue
Chicago, IL 60611
Phone: 800-621-8738
Fax: 312-329-8882
Web site: www.crb.com

Counselors of Real Estate
430 North Michigan Avenue
Chicago, IL 60611
Phone: 312-219-8427
Web site: www.cre.org

Environmental Law Institute
1616 P Street, NW, Suite 200
Washington, DC 20036
Phone: 202-939-3800
Fax: 202-939-3868
Web site: www.eli.org

Federation of Associations of
Regulatory Boards
1603 Orrington Avenue, Suite 2080
Evanston, IL 60201

Phone: 847-328-7909
Fax: 847-864-0588
Web site: www.farb.org

Foundation of Real Estate
    Appraisers
4907 Morena Boulevard, Suite 1415
San Diego, CA 92117
Phone: 800-882-4410
Fax: 858-273-8026
Web site: www.frea.com

Institute of Real Estate Management
430 North Michigan Avenue
Chicago, IL 60611
Phone: 312-329-6000
Fax: 312-661-0217
Web site: www.irem.org

International Association of
    Assessing Officers
130 East Randolph Street, Suite 850
Chicago, IL 60601
Phone: 312-819-6100
Fax: 312-819-6149
Web site: www.iaao.org

International Business Brokers
    Association
401 North Michigan Avenue,
    Suite 2200
Chicago, IL 60611
Phone: 888-686-4222
Fax: 312-673-6599
Web site: www.ibba.org

International City/County
    Management Association
777 North Capitol Street, NE,
    Suite 500
Washington, DC 20002
Phone: 202-289-4262
Fax: 202-962-3500
Web site: www.icma.org

International Real Estate Institute
1224 North Nokomis Northeast
Alexandria, MN 56308
Phone: 320-763-4648
Fax: 320-763-9290
Web site: www.iami.org/irei.cfm

International Real Property
    Foundation
700 11th Street, NW, Suite 550
Washington, DC 20001
Phone: 202-383-1296
Fax: 202-383-7549

Land Development Institute, Ltd.
1401 16th Street, NW
Washington, DC 20036
Phone: 202-232-2144

Mortgage Bankers Association of
    America
1919 Pennsylvania Avenue, NW
Washington, DC 20006
Phone: 800-793-6222 or 202-557-2700
Fax: 202-721-0247
Web site: www.mbaa.org

National Apartment Association
201 North Union Street, Suite 200
Alexandria, VA 22314
Phone: 703-518-6141
Web site: www.naahq.org

National Association of Exclusive
    Buyer Agents
320 West Sabal Palm Place, Suite 150
Longwood, FL 32779
Phone: 407-767-7700
Fax: 407-834-4747
Web site: www.naeba.org

National Association of Hispanic
    Real Estate Professionals
1650 Hotel Circle North, Suite 215A
San Diego, CA 92108

Phone: 800-964-5373
Fax: 619-209-4773

National Association of Home
   Builders
1201 15th Street, NW
Washington, DC 20005
Phone: 800-368-5242
Fax: 202-822-0559
Web site: www.nahb.org

National Association of Independent
   Fee Appraisers
7501 Murdoch Avenue
St. Louis, MO 63119
Phone: 314-781-6688
Fax: 314-781-2872
Web site: www.naifa.com

National Association of Insurance
   Commissioners
2301 McGee, Suite 800
Kansas City, MO 64108
Phone: 816-842-3600
Web site: www.naic.org

National Association of Master
   Appraisers
P.O. Box 12617
San Antonio, TX 78212
Phone: 512-271-0781

National Association of Mortgage
   Brokers
8201 Greensboro Drive, Suite 300
McLean, VA 22102
Phone: 703-610-9009
Fax: 703-610-9005
Web site: www.namb.org

National Association of Real Estate
   Appraisers
1224 North Nokomis Northeast
Alexandria, MN 56308
Phone: 320-763-7626

Fax: 320-763-9290
Web site: www.iami.org/narea.cfm

National Association of Real Estate
   Brokers
1629 K Street, NW, Suite 602
Washington, DC 20006
Phone: 202-785-4477
Fax: 202-785-1244
Web site: www.nareb.com

National Association of Real Estate
   Companies
P.O. Box 958
Columbia, MD 21044
Phone: 410-992-6476
Fax: 410-992-6363
Web site: www.narec.org

National Association of Real Estate
   Investment Fiduciaries
2 Prudential Plaza
180 North Stetson Avenue,
   Suite 2515
Chicago, IL 60601
Phone: 312-819-5890
Fax: 312-819-5891
Web site: www.ncreif.org

National Association of Real Estate
   Investment Trusts, Inc.
1875 Eye Street, Suite 600
Washington, DC 20006
Phone: 800-3-NAREIT
Fax: 202-739-9401
Web site: www.nareit.com

National Association of Real Estate
   Professionals
2950 East Flamingo Road, Suite D-1
Las Vegas, NV 89123
Phone: 702-862-4001
Fax: 702-862-8065
Web site: www.narep.net

National Association of Realtors
430 North Michigan Avenue
Chicago, IL 60611
Phone: 800-874-6500
Web site: www.nar.realtor.com

National Association of Review
    Appraisers & Mortgage
    Underwriters
1224 North Nokomis Northeast
Alexandria, MN 56308
Phone: 320-763-7626
Fax: 320-763-9290
Web site: www.iami.org/nara.cfm

National Board of Certification for
    Community Association
    Managers
P.O. Box 25037
Alexandria, VA 22313
Phone: 703-836-6902
Fax: 703-548-9543
Web site: www.nbccam.org

National Council of Exchangers
13410 East Cypress Forest Drive
Houston, TX 77070
Phone: 713-849-8411

National Land Council
P.O. Box 3106
Tallahassee, FL 32315
Phone: 850-222-2563
Fax: 850-224-2406

Property Management Association
8811 Colesville Road, Suite G106
Silver Spring, MD 20910
Phone: 301-597-6543

Real Estate Educators Association
401 Wekiva Springs Road, Suite 241
Longwood, FL 32779
Phone: 407-834-6688
Fax: 407-834-4747

Web site: www.reea.com

Realtors Land Institute
430 North Michigan Avenue,
    Suite 400
Chicago, IL 60611
Phone: 800-441-LAND
Fax: 312-329-8633
Web site: www.rliland.com

Residential Sales Council
430 North Michigan Avenue
Chicago, IL 60611
Phone: 312-329-3780

Urban Land Institute
1025 Thomas Jefferson Street, NE,
    Suite 500 West
Washington, DC 20007
Phone: 202-624-7000
Fax: 202-624-7140
Web site: www.uli.org

Women's Council of Realtors
430 North Michigan Avenue
Chicago, IL 60611
Phone: 312-329-8483
Web site: www.wcr.org

Consumer Advocacy Groups Online

AARP
Phone: 800-424-3410
Web site: www.aarp.org

American Council of Consumer
    Interests
Phone: 573-882-3817
Web site:
    www.consumerinterests.org

Consumers International
Web site:
    www.consumersinternational.org

Fair Housing Network
Web site: www.fairhousing.org

National Housing Trust
Web site: www.nhtinc.org

Federal Agencies

Environmental Protection Agency
401 M Street, SW
Washington, DC 20460
Phone: 202-233-9431
Fax: 202-233-9652
Web site: www.epa.gov

Federal Trade Commission
600 Pennsylvania Avenue, NW
Washington, DC 20580
Phone: 202-326-2000
Web site: www.ftc.gov

U.S. Department of Housing & Urban
    Development
451 7th Street, SW, Room 5235
Washington, DC 20410
Phone: 202-708-1992, ext. 321
Web site: www.hud.gov

State Real Estate Boards

Alabama Real Estate Commission
1201 Carmichael Way
Montgomery, AL 36106
Phone: 334-242-5544
Fax: 334-270-9118
Web site: www.arec.state.al.us

Alabama Home Builders Licensure
    Board
400 South Union Street, Suite 195
Montgomery, AL 36130
Phone: 334-242-2230

Fax: 334-263-1397
Web site: www.agencies.state.al.us/
    homebuilders

Alabama Licensing Board for
    General Contractors
2525 Fairlane Drive
Montgomery, AL 36116
Web site: www.agencies.state.al.us/
    gencontrbd

Alaska Division of Occupational
    Licensing
Real Estate Commission
3601 C Street, Suite 722
Anchorage, AK 99503
Phone: 907-269-8160
Fax: 907-269-8156
Web site: www.dced.state.ak.us/occ/
    prec.htm

Arizona Department of Real
    Estate
2910 North 44th Street, Suite 100
Phoenix, AZ 85018
Phone: 602-468-1414
Fax: 602-468-0562
Web site: www.re.state.az.us

Arizona Registrar of Contractors
800 West Washington, 6th Floor
Phoenix, AZ 85007
Phone: 602-542-1525
Fax: 602-542-1536
Web site: www.rc.state.az.us

Arkansas Real Estate Commission
612 South Summit Street
Little Rock, AR 72201
Phone: 501-683-0810
Fax: 501-683-8020
Web site: www.state.ar.us/arec/
    arecweb.html

Arkansas Contractors Licensing
  Board
4100 Richards Road
North Little Rock, AR 72117
Phone: 501-372-4661
Fax: 501-372-2247
Web site: www.state.ar.us/clb

Arkansas HVACR Licensing Board
4815 West Markham Street, Slot 24
Little Rock, AR 72205
Phone: 501-661-2642
Fax: 501-661-2671

California Department of Real
  Estate
P.O. Box 187000
Sacramento, CA 95818
Phone: 916-227-0864 or 916-227-0931
Web site: www.dre.ca.gov

California Contractors License
  Board
P.O. Box 26000
Sacramento, CA 95826
Phone: 916-255-4000
Fax: 916-364-0130
Web site: www.cslb.ca.gov

Colorado Department of Regulatory
  Agencies
Division of Real Estate
1900 Grant Street, Suite 600
Denver, CO 80203
Phone: 303-894-2166
Fax: 303-894-2683
Web site: www.dora.state.co.us/
  real-estate

Connecticut Department of
  Consumer Protection
Occupational and Professional
  Licensing Division
165 Capitol Avenue, Room 110

Hartford, CT 06106
Phone: 860-713-6150
Fax: 860-713-7239
Web site: www.state.ct.us/dcp

Delaware Real Estate Commission
861 Silver Lake Boulevard, Suite 203
Dover, DE 19904
Phone: 302-739-4522, ext. 219
Fax: 302-739-2711
Web site:
  www.professionallicensing.
  state.de.us/boards/realestate

Florida Division of Real Estate
400 West Robinson Street,
  Suite N309 (P.O. Box 1900)
Orlando, FL 32802
Phone: 407-245-0800
Fax: 407-245-0800
Web site: www.state.fl.us/dbpr/re/

Florida Construction Industry
  Licensing Board
1940 North Monroe Street, Suite 33
Tallahassee, FL 32399
Phone: 850-487-1395
Web site:
  www.state.fl.us/dbpr/pro/cilb/

Florida Electrical Contractors'
  Licensing Board
1940 North Monroe Street, Suite 60
Tallahassee, FL 32399
Phone: 850-487-1395
Fax: 850-922-2918
Web site:
  www.state.fl.us/dbpr/pro/elboard/

Georgia Real Estate Commission
Suite 1000—International Tower
229 Peachtree Street Northeast
Atlanta, GA 30303
Phone: 404-656-3916

Fax: 404-656-6650
Web site: www.grec.state.ga.us

Georgia Construction Industry
  Licensing Board
237 Coliseum Drive
Macon, GA 31217
Phone: 478-207-1416
Fax: 478-207-1425
Web site: www.sos.state.ga.us/plb/
  construct/

Hawaii Contractors Licensing
  Board
P.O. Box 3469
Honolulu, HI 96801
Phone: 808-586-2700
Fax: 808-586-2689
Web site: www.state.hi.us/dcca/pvl/

Idaho Real Estate Commission
P.O. Box 83720
Boise, ID 83720
Phone: 208-334-3285
Fax: 208-334-2050
Web site: www2.state.id.us/irec/

Illinois Office of Banks and Real
  Estate
500 East Monroe Street, Suite 200
Springfield, IL 62701
Phone: 217-785-9300
Fax: 217-782-3390
Web site: www.state.il.us/obr

Indiana Professional Licensing
  Agency
302 West Washington Street,
  Room E034
Indianapolis, IN 46204
Phone: 317-232-2980
Fax: 317-232-2312
Web site:
  www.in.gov/pla/bandc/estate

Iowa Real Estate Commission
1918 Southeast Hulsizer Avenue
Ankeny, IA 50021
Phone: 515-281-3183
Fax: 515-281-7411
Web site: www.state.ia.us/
  government/com/prof/realesta/

Kansas Real Estate Commission
3 Townsite Plaza, Suite 200
120 Southeast 6th Avenue
Topeka, KS 66603
Phone: 785-296-3411
Fax: 785-296-1771
Web site: www.ink.org/public/krec

Kentucky Real Estate Commission
10200 Linn Station Road, Suite 201
Louisville, KY 40223
Phone: 502-425-4273
Fax: 502-426-2717
Web site: www.krec.net

Kentucky Department of Housing,
  Building & Construction
1047 Highway 127 South, Suite 1
Frankfort, KY 40601
Phone: 502-564-8044
Fax: 502-564-3833

Louisiana Real Estate Commission
P.O. Box 14785
Baton Rouge, LA 70898
Phone: 225-925-4771
Fax: 225-925-4431
Web site: www.lrec.state.la.us

Louisiana Licensing Board for
  Contractors
P.O. Box 14419
Baton Rouge, LA 70898
Phone: 225-765-2301 or 800-256-1392
Fax: 225-765-2431
Web site: www.lslbc.state.la.us

Maine Real Estate Commission
35 State House Station
Augusta, ME 04333
Phone: 207-624-8603
Fax: 207-624-8637
Web site: www.state.me.us/
pfr/led/rec/

Maryland Real Estate Commission
500 North Calvert Street
Baltimore, MD 21202
Phone: 410-230-6200
Fax: 410-333-0023
Web site: www.dllr.state.md.us/
license/real_est/

Maryland Home Improvement
Commission
500 North Calvert Street, Room 306
Baltimore, MD 21202
Phone: 410-230-6176
Fax: 410-333-0851
Web site: www.dllr.state.md.us/
license/home_imprv/

Massachusetts Real Estate Board
239 Causeway Street, Suite 500
Boston, MA 02114
Phone: 617-727-2373
Fax: 617-727-2669
Web site: www.state.ma.us/reg/

Michigan Department of Consumer
& Industry Services
Bureau of Commercial Services
P.O. Box 30243
Lansing, MI 48909
Phone: 517-241-9288
Fax: 517-241-9280
Web site: www.cis.state.mi.us

Michigan Department of Consumer
& Industry Services

Bureau of Commercial Services—
Builders Unit
P.O. Box 30018
Lansing, MI 48909
Phone: 517-241-9244
Fax: 517-241-9280
Web site: www.cis.state.mi.us/bcs/
builders/

Minnesota Department of
Commerce
85 East 7th Place
St. Paul, MN 55101
Phone: 651-296-6025
Fax: 651-282-2568
Web site: www.commerce.state.
mn.us

Mississippi Real Estate Commission
P.O. Box 12685
Jackson, MS 39236
Phone: 601-932-9191
Fax: 601-932-2990
Web site: www.mrec.state.ms.us

Mississippi State Board of
Contractors
215 Woodline Drive, Suite B
Jackson, MS 39232
Phone: 601-354-6161
Fax: 601-354-6715
Web site: www.msboc.state.ms.us

Missouri Real Estate Commission
P.O. Box 1339
3605 Missouri Boulevard
Jefferson City, MO 65102
Phone: 573-751-2628
Fax: 573-751-2777
Web site: www.ecodev.state.mo.us/
pr/restate/

Montana Board of Realty Regulation
P.O. Box 200513

301 South Park
Helena, MT 59620
Phone: 406-444-2961
Fax: 406-841-2323
Web site:
  www.discoveringmontana.com/
  dli/rre/

Montana Department of Labor &
  Industry
Contractor Registration
P.O. Box 8011
Helena, MT 59604
Phone: 406-444-9586

Nebraska Real Estate Commission
P.O. Box 94667
Lincoln, NE 68509
Phone: 402-471-2004
Fax: 402-471-4492
Web site: www.nol.org/home/NREC/

Nevada Department of Business &
  Industry
Real Estate Division
2501 East Sahara Avenue, Suite 102
Las Vegas, NV 89104
Phone: 702-486-4033
Fax: 702-486-4275
Web site: www.red.state.nv.us

Nevada Contractors Board
2310 Corporate Circle, Suite 200
Henderson, NV 89074
Phone: 702-486-1100
Fax: 702-486-1190
Web site: www.nscb.state.nv.us

New Hampshire Real Estate
  Commission
State House Annex
25 Capitol Street, Room 435
Concord, NH 03301
Phone: 603-271-2701

Fax: 603-271-1039
Web site: www.state.nh.us/nhrec

New Jersey Real Estate Commission
20 West State Street
P.O. Box 328
Trenton, NJ 08625
Phone: 609-292-8280
Fax: 609-292-0944
Web site: www.naic.org/nj/realcom/

New Mexico Real Estate
  Commission
1650 University Boulevard
Northeast, Suite 490
Albuquerque, NM 87102
Phone: 800-801-7505 or 505-841-9120
Fax: 505-246-0725
Web site: www.state.nm.us/clients/
  nmrec/

New Mexico Construction Industries
  Division
P.O. Box 25101
Sante Fe, NM 87504
Phone: 919-733-9042
Fax: 919-733-6105
Web site: www.rid.state.nm.us/cid/

New York Division of Licensing
  Services
84 Holland Avenue
Albany, NY 12208
Phone: 518-473-2728
Fax: 518-473-2730
Web site: www.dos.state.ny.us/lcns/

North Carolina Real Estate
  Commission
P.O. Box 17100
Raleigh, NC 27619
Phone: 919-875-3700
Fax: 919-872-0038
Web site: www.ncrec.state.nc.us

North Carolina Board of Examiners
of Plumbing, Heating & Fire
Sprinkler Contractors
1109 Dresser Court
Raleigh, NC 27609
Phone: 919-875-3612
Fax: 919-875-3616
Web site: www.nclicensing.org

North Carolina Licensing Board for
General Contractors
P.O. Box 17187
Raleigh, NC 27619
Phone: 919-571-4183
Fax: 919-571-4703
Web site: www.nclbgc.com

North Carolina State Board of
Examiners of Electrical
Contractors
P.O. Box 18727
Raleigh, NC 27619
Phone: 919-733-9042
Fax: 919-733-6105
Web site: www.ncbeec.org

North Dakota Real Estate
Commission
314 East Thayer Avenue
P.O. Box 727
Bismarck, ND 58502
Phone: 701-328-9749
Fax: 701-328-9750

Ohio Division of Real Estate and
Professional Licensing
77 South High Street, 20th Floor
Columbus, OH 43215
Phone: 614-466-4100
Fax: 614-644-0584
Web site: www.com.state.oh.us/real/

Oklahoma Real Estate Commission
Shepherd Mall

2401 Northwest 23rd Street,
Suite 18
Oklahoma City, OK 73107
Phone: 405-521-3387
Fax: 405-521-2189
Web site: www.orec.state.ok.us

Oregon Real Estate Agency
1177 Center Street Northeast
Salem, OR 97301
Phone: 503-378-4170
Fax: 503-378-2491
Web site: www.rea.state.or.us

Oregon Construction Contractors
Board
P.O. Box 14140
Salem, OR 97309
Phone: 503-378-4621
Fax: 503-373-2007
Web site: www.ccb.state.or.us

Pennsylvania Real Estate
Commission
P.O. Box 2649
Harrisburg, PA 17105
Phone: 717-783-3658
Fax: 717-787-0250
Web site: www.dos.state.pa.us/
bpoa/recomm/

Rhode Island Department of
Business Regulation
233 Richmond Street, Suite 230
Providence, RI 02903
Phone: 401-222-2255
Fax: 401-222-6654
Web site: www.rilin.state.ri.us

Rhode Island Contractors'
Registration Board
1 Capitol Hill
Providence, RI 02908
Phone: 401-222-1268

Fax: 401-222-2599
Web site: www.crb.state.ri.us

South Carolina Department of Labor
Licensing & Regulation
Real Estate Commission
P.O. Box 11847
Columbia, SC 29211
Phone: 803-896-4404
Fax: 803-896-4400
Web site: www.llr.state.sc.us/POL/
RealEstateCommission/

South Carolina Contractors'
Licensing Board
P.O. Box 11329
Columbia, SC 29211
Phone: 803-896-4686
Fax: 803-896-4364
Web site: www.llr.state.sc.us/POL/
Contractors/

South Carolina Residential Builders
Commission
P.O. Box 11329
Columbia, SC 29211
Phone: 803-896-4696
Fax: 803-896-4656
Web site: www.llr.state.sc.us/POL/
ResidentialBuilders/

South Dakota Real Estate
Commission
118 West Capitol
Pierre, SD 57501
Phone: 605-773-3600
Fax: 605-773-4356
Web site: www.state.sd.us/state/
executive/dcr/realestate/

Tennessee Real Estate Commission
500 James Robertson Parkway
Davy Crockett Tower, Suite 180
Nashville, TN 37243

Phone: 615-741-2273
Fax: 615-741-0313
Web site: www.state.tn.us/
commerce/trec/

Tennessee Board for Licensing
General Contractors
500 James Robertson Parkway,
Suite 110
Nashville, TN 37243
Phone: 800-544-7693 or 615-741-8307
Fax: 615-532-2868

Texas Real Estate Commission
P.O. Box 12188
Austin, TX 78711
Phone: 512-465-3900
Fax: 512-465-3910
Web site: www.trec.state.tx.us

Texas Department of Licensing &
Regulation
P.O. Box 12157
Austin, TX 78711
Phone: 512-463-7369
Fax: 512-475-2872
Web site: www.license.state.tx.us/
acr/acr.htm

Utah Division of Real Estate
P.O. Box 146711
Salt Lake City, UT 84114
Phone: 801-530-6747
Fax: 801-530-6749
Web site:
www.commerce.utah.gov/dre

Utah Construction Trades Bureau
Division of Occupational &
Professional Licensing
P.O. Box 146741
Salt Lake City, UT 84114
Phone: 801-530-6628
Fax: 801-530-6511

Web site: www.dopl.utah.gov/
licensing/contractor.html

Vermont Office of Professional
Regulation
Real Estate Commission
81 River Street, Drawer 9
Montpelier, VT 05609
Phone: 802-828-3228
Fax: 802-828-2368
Web site: www.sec.state.vt.us

Virginia Department of
Professional and
Occupational Regulation
3600 West Broad Street
Richmond, VA 23230
Phone: 804-367-8526
Fax: 804-367-2475
Web site: www.state.va.us/dpor

Virginia Board of Contractors
3600 West Broad Street, 4th Floor
Richmond, VA 23230
Phone: 804-367-8511
Fax: 804-367-6295
Web site: www.state.va.us/dpor

Washington Department of
Licensing
Business and Professions Division,
Real Estate
P.O. Box 9015
Olympia, WA 98507
Phone: 360-753-2262
Fax: 360-586-0998
Web site: www.wa.gov.dol/bpd/
refront.htm

Washington Department of Labor &
Industries
P.O. Box 44450
Olympia, WA 98504
Phone: 360-902-6303

Fax: 360-902-6040
Web site: www.lni.wa.gov

West Virginia Real Estate
Commission
1033 Quarrier Street, Suite 400
Charleston, WV 25301
Phone: 304-558-3555
Fax: 304-558-6442
Web site: www.state.wv.us/wvrec

West Virginia Contractors Licensing
Board—Division of Labor
Capitol Complex, Building 6,
Room B-749
Charleston, WV 25305
Phone: 304-558-7890
Fax: 304-558-3797
Web site: www.state.wv.us/labor/
contractor/

Wyoming Real Estate Commission
2020 Carey Avenue, Suite 100
Cheyenne, WY 82002
Phone: 307-777-7141
Fax: 307-777-3796
Web site:
www.realestate.state.wy.us

Books

*100 Questions Every First-Time Home
Buyer Should Ask,* second edition.
Glink, Ilyce. New York: Random
House, 2000.

Buying or Selling a Home. Chicago,
IL: National Association of Realtors,
2001.

*The Complete Idiot's Guide to Building
Your Own Home.* Ramsey, Dan.
Indianapolis: Alpha Books, 2002.

Dictionary of Real Estate Terms, fifth edition. Hauppauge, NY: Barron's Educational Series, Inc., 2000.

Realty Bluebook, 32nd edition. Chicago: Dearborn Financial Publishing, Inc., 2000.

Starting Out. Hymer, Dian. San Francisco: Chronicle Books, 1997.

Tips and Traps When Buying a Home. Irwin, Robert. New York: McGraw-Hill, 1997.

What the "Experts" May Not Tell You About Building or Renovating Your Home. Johnston, Amy. New York: Warner Books, 2003.

Your Dream Home: A Comprehensive Guide to Buying a House, Condo, or Coop. Smith, Marguerite. New York: Warner Books, 1997.

Additional books on real estate topics are available online at www.mulligan books.com.

Index

About the Author

Dan Ramsey first became a licensed real estate agent more than twenty-five years ago. After a successful sales career, he authored thirty-plus books for real estate investors, building contractors, and homeowners. Today he is a building and re-modeling contractor in northern California. Dan knows how to save thousands of dollars when buying a home—with tips your agent, lender, or escrow officer may not tell you.

**LOOK FOR THE OTHER BOOKS IN THIS SERIES
WHAT THE "EXPERTS" MAY NOT TELL YOU ABOUT™...**

BUILDING OR RENOVATING YOUR HOME

❏

CAR REPAIR

❏

GROWING THE PERFECT LAWN